The
Unused Potential
of Marriage
and Sex

The Unused Potential of Marriage and Sex

BETTY GROVER EISNER

LITTLE, BROWN AND COMPANY • BOSTON • TORONTO

To those I love:

Tuesday's children and their matrix;
Wednesday's children and their motion;
And La Mesa's loves — Bill, Maleah, and D.B.

Contents

Contents

The Unused Potential of Marriage and Sex

1

The Dilemma of Marriage
and Modern Man

THE institution of marriage arose out of the physical necessity to keep men and women together long enough to produce and raise enough children to continue the race. Monogamy (or carefully prescribed multiple marriages in situations of critical shortages of members of either sex) makes procreation more likely by increasing the probability and consistency of intercourse.

Marriage is also a means of guaranteeing security and continuity for the infant long enough for him to survive physically on his own. It creates a stable environment for child rearing and extends the number of learning years. The longer the learning years, the more fully the accumulated knowledge of the family, the tribe, and the race can be transferred to the next generation. Although today the task of teaching the young has been progressively usurped by the state and some churches (mainly through parental default), the primary vehicle for the transfer of culture remains the family.

More recently, since the Renaissance, marriage has had to provide a working arrangement for two people for the mutual satisfaction of their needs. Specifically, marriage is supposed to provide both rewarding and exclusive sex for its partners at a time when the pressure toward sexual variety and experimentation is at high tide.

Marriage is also expected to provide companionship — quite possibly for two very different people — and even more important, the opportunity for growth and fulfillment of the creative potential of both.

Also, as an added last and almost insurmountable burden, one's marriage partner today is called on to help alleviate the tensions of a world in the Atomic Age of Anxiety — the pressures and strains created by a world torn by strife and rushing toward what appears to be certain self-annihilation.

Any one of these requirements — let alone all of them — is a giant-sized order for any institution.

As if that weren't enough, the rules of property and inheritance hitched onto marriage like a caboose — which grew and grew.

Today society is an interrelated network of rigidities of behavior. It is an intricate and restrictive structure of complicated institutions and outworn customs and traditions. The resulting grand rigidity is so much a part of behavioral patterns that evolutionary change is impossible; institutions and patterns and morals and mores must be shattered in order to be escaped.

At the same time mankind is threatened with the possibility of self-extinction by two tiny bits of matter — the atom and the fertilized human ovum — both in the process of explosion.

Pressure to escape arises — particularly with the younger generation who find their environment in a violent state of upheaval which cannot be handled by inflexible institutions. Man seeks to find meaning — in himself and in relationship — and he looks first and most often to sex and to a continuing relationship of depth to find an answer.

When he first appeared on this blue planet of earth it was a life and death matter for man to procreate and multiply. Today the problem is reversed: man must find a means other than war to halt the exponential increase of his species.

Because of this necessity to constrain rather than to multiply there is implicit a basic, almost complete, reversal in the foundation of marriage and a transformation in the relationship between men and women. These shifts have shaken the structure of society itself — a society which wasn't too stable anyway because of the other changes imposed by our rapidly developing material sciences.

These shifts have all come so rapidly that there has not been time to understand them — let alone to restructure marriage and society on a more realistic basis. Nor has there been any opportunity to change the marriage relationship to one less geared to procreation and more oriented toward companionship and continued maturation for the years which science has added to man's span of life. This leaves a gap between what is and what might be in the relations between men and women and the relationship of marriage — an unused potential both in marriage and in sex.

Just what can be done about all this is not clear. In some instances the very nature of what is necessary — or why or how much — is obscure. But time is running out.

With the threat of annihilation in the background, men and women won't wait — nor especially will boys and girls. When evolutionary changes fail to materialize, revolutionary changes take place. Revolutionary changes are in process today throughout all of society, and some of them are extremely violent. Revolutionary changes are also at work on the relationship between men and women. And human beings are caught in the disparity between the potential and the actual.

It appears that the dilemma in which the institution of marriage finds itself today is also the dilemma of modern man: too many impossible demands from too many sources — all of which clamor for immediate and often simultaneous solution at a time when man has no knowledge of who he is and where he is going, no sense of whole identity and meaningful goal.

It is beyond the realm of possibility to expect fulfillment of all the demands which the institution of marriage has been called upon to manage.

What is to be done?

2

Relationship of Men to Women

ALL of the special and extraordinary needs and demands which marriage and modern man are called on to solve revolve around the relationship of a man with a woman. At this point in time, the equilibrium between the sexes is in as wild a fluctuation as their standards of behavior.

It is important, in the attempt to understand modern man and modern marriage, to examine briefly the story of their interaction. Historically, the pattern of relationship between men and women was built on differences arising from their differing biological roles and on women's physical inferiority to man. In primitive times, woman's slighter, less muscular build and her function of childbearing usually restricted her to duties inside the family dwelling. There was a division of labor between the procuring of food and protection on the one hand, and the preparation of food and the care of the family on the other.

With the shift from hunting and gathering to tilling of soil, and with the domestication of animals, physical prowess became less important, and with industrialization and urbanization, the last vestiges of man's need to hunt for food and personally to repulse enemies disappeared. Today, with the help of machines, women can perform most tasks as well as men (small, repetitive ones even better), and physical prowess or superior strength has very little to do with superior performance outside the realm of sports.

Society has reflected this change: in the highly industrialized countries the status of women has shifted from that of inferior chattels to a more equal footing with men. It has remained relatively unchanged only in primitive countries, where the "inferior" status of women has been embedded into the fabric of society by early codification of basic laws on individual rights, marriage, and property. This inequity is bound to shift more toward equilibrium in the coming years because of the interrelatedness of all peoples and all countries on the planet.*

---

* Swiss women are still fighting for the right to vote (Los Angeles *Times*, February 26, 1969); women in Britain were first offered the same pay as men in February of 1969 (Los Angeles *Times*, February 13, 1969), two years later than in the U.S.; in October of 1968 there was a suit in court to allow airline stewardesses on a certain airline to marry (all male personnel have had no prohibition with respect to marriage) (Los Angeles *Times*, October 29, 1969); and a crusading California woman had a suit before the Supreme Court to allow women to work beyond the eight-hour maximum if necessary. Two and a half months later a Tacoma, Washington, woman brought suit for the right to sit at the bar in a cocktail lounge (Los Angeles *Times*, January 10, 1969).

However, in many Oriental countries and a large part of Africa women are still considered chattels without legal rights, and even in European countries there are restrictions and limitations. It was in late November of 1968 that a Sicilian girl defied the code of the island which forced a girl who had been abducted and raped to marry her abductor or be virtually outcast (she married the man she loved). In male-dominated countries as modern as Scotland and Greece it is not appropriate for women to drink in public; women seen in pubs and sidewalk cafes there are tourists.

However, even in industrialized societies pockets of formalized discrimination based on the historical concept of masculine supremacy and fossilized mores from primitive nomadic and agrarian societies are found where eddies occur apart from the mainstream of social change. Examples of this fossilized backwash are to be found mainly in primitive countries, inaccessible areas, fundamentalist religions, and rigid institutions such as the Catholic Church. If there is any doubt about the archaic concepts of the Catholic Church concerning the status of women, one need only be reminded of their unrealistic stand against birth control, note the Father, Son, and Holy Ghost of the Trinity (also by legacy in most Protestant churches), count the number of women priests, cardinals and bishops, and rejoice in the fact that at least in this century Mary was recognized as elevated into heaven to join God and Jesus.

Shift of Equilibrium

The trend toward equality between the sexes has been vastly speeded by the appearance of new and easy contraceptive methods which have given women voluntary control over the childbearing role. With this freedom,

---

It is interesting to note that in some cases, particularly in the United States where liberal labor, divorce, and inheritance laws protecting women have been enacted, there has been what appears to be overcompensation toward overprotection of women and actual penalization of men (cf. California divorce laws). The bulk of wealth in the United States — over three-quarters of it — is in women's names, a direct reversal from a hundred years ago. And in highly industrialized countries with a shortage of labor, such as Russia, women not only occupy their proportional share of professional jobs, such as doctors and engineers and one Cosmonaut, but also they share equally in heavy physical jobs, such as construction, garbage collection, and street repair.

and with the relaxation of traditions barring them from work outside the home, women have been liberated from financial dependency on and domination by men.

As the equilibrium between male and female has shifted, there have been dislocations in everything from economic patterns (women generally buy differently from men) to the constitution of the family (with elimination of the elderly), resulting in turbulence in individual relationships. Further, there are disruptions from social mobility, and a present-day marriage may have to survive the shift of either the husband — or the wife — several notches up or down in the economic or social ladder.

As the equilibrium has swung, sometimes past the balance point, at times and in places there have been gyrations which have displaced the fulcrum toward women. This has occurred most frequently in middle-class American society. This excessive displacement toward women is just as destructive as the prior displacement toward men: in fact, disequilibrium in either direction (toward male or female) is profoundly to be avoided.

However, the center of equilibrium should not be fixed at any one point: ideally, balance consists of a series of changing equilibriums, shifting according to the specific ongoing activity. Control or the main burden of responsibility and authority for any particular activity should not depend on gender but on who is most suited to handle the situation.

Such flexibility of the center of gravity of a marriage relationship is very difficult to achieve. It presupposes flexibility and maturity of adaptation in the two individuals, and the capacity to play either a male or female role. It entails the maturity necessary to put aside games of control and manipulation in the service of responding to any situation which arises with the action appropriate to the situation rather than the action which "feels" best to the individual or the one which most lowers anxiety. For instance, in cases of illness of the mother, the father should be able to feed and care for the children; when a father is incapacitated, the mother should be able to step out and take a job to help out with temporary income. If the husband has demanding work, time requirements might be best met by having the wife handle the budget, money, and maybe even income tax returns; certainly any husband and father should be willing to pitch in and do part of the housework if his wife is also working or in case of any unusual situation.

Today we see our young people pushing vigorously in the direction of blurring the distinctions between men and women, the most apparent examples being in the area of personal appearance: longer hair for boys, shorter hair for girls and pants for everybody. The breakdown in differences of roles is also seen in choice of vocation, in the opening of sexual freedom to girls as well as to boys, and in a new type of cooperative relationship between young people. However, the maturational necessity involved in a flexible equilibrium between two parties to a marriage contract goes far beyond personal appearance or choice of job or sexual partners.

There is also the very real difficulty that it has become progressively more difficult for both men and women to find satisfaction in their roles as civilization has become more mechanized and complicated and the distinctions between formerly unique roles have disappeared (except in childbearing). This certainly is more a fault of society than a default of the individual, but it is none the less painful.

Historically, man is the aggressor, the provider, and protector — woman the creator, the sustainer, the restorer. When a man had a forest to clear, food to hunt and a family to protect, the roots of his being were nourished by the urgency and importance of the tasks he performed and the skill with which he performed them. Women, in turn, found their fulfillment in the rearing of the children, as helpmates to their men, and in the joy of the successful completion of the necessary tasks involved in making a household (cave, cottage, or castle) function smoothly and well.

How different today!

Today the average man performs a task which is only a small part of a large operation whose overall pattern is apparent to only a fraction of the management in the company where he works. He is constantly threatened by layoffs, unemployment, or automation. Often his wife works (subject to the same conditions as he) and she may earn nearly as much as he does or possibly even more if she has a special skill. How adequate can a man feel as provider under circumstances such as these?

Further, how much of a man's role as protector is left to him when on the one hand federal, state, and local governments take care of keeping the peace but on the other hand no one is able to maintain peace against possible atomic annihilation? Also, with the recent increase of civil disorder, protection of life and property can't always be guaranteed by governmental agencies, but there is very little the individual can do about the critical situation on his own without himself breaking laws. Modern man is

almost helpless with respect to using his own physical
strength to provide the direct insurance that his family's
needs are met — or even to insure the survival of a world
where there is hope that they can be met.

As a footnote to the erosion of performance of the protective function, witness the number of crimes of violence
committed in full view of people who could have at least
attempted to interfere but did not step one foot forward
to help.

With respect to women's changing role, the rigors of
pregnancy and childbirth have been tempered by modern
medicine; household tasks have been simplified and
many eliminated by machines and gadgets; individuals
and agencies can be found to care for children at any
time. All to the good: why should any individual suffer
needlessly or work herself to a frazzle when there is an
easier way? After all, the deep creative surge and satisfaction is in caring for — taking care of, caring about — a
husband and children and not in the pain of production
or the weariness of extra work.

But what happens to a woman's feeling of adequacy
after the toddler days are over, and the burden of convey-
ing the accumulated wisdom of the culture and its mores
has been transferred to the waiting hands of church,
school, and state? At this time the husband is usually
established in his work, and a woman feels useless on
many counts — a state probably unknown in primitive
times when the rigors of everyday life saw to it that no
one lived long enough to outgrow their usefulness.

A further blow today is that just at the time a woman
is losing her role as nurturing mother, her actual capacity
to become a mother dwindles to termination. It is a

double blow: no one really needs her any longer as a physical mother — just when she is ceasing to be able to become one. Small wonder that modern woman's "change of life" becomes a basic identity crisis and demands a *real* change of life in the capacity to shift roles and find new ones in a society which itself is undergoing its own "point of no return" crisis.

Further, a wife also suffers from the same fears of losing security as her husband — economic, social, psychological security, even including possible loss of life from an atomic war. Neither the husband nor the wife can change the fact of the possibility of atomic annihilation with its accompanying anxiety. Both feel insecure, frustrated, and inadequate, and the wife feels her burden doubly because she — as sustainer and supporter — should be helping her husband carry the load of his tensions and anxieties as well as carrying her own.

How much greater a frustration if she feels that she is failing him as well as herself.

Load Carrying as a Role

There is an added function husband and wife perform for each other which is not widely recognized or understood. Historically it has been more the function of the wife as sustainer and supporter of the household (and especially of her husband). Almost daily the creative wife helps alleviate her husband's tensions: tensions from the boss or a difficult day's work and any feelings of inadequacy and frustration with respect to his creativity and production on the job. She does this in a number of ways: by maintaining a "haven" for him at home; by being listener, guardian of guilt, provider of beer, titillater

of the palate, restorer of adequacy through affection and
sex, and in many other ways. By helping share and discharge his load, she lightens his burdens. In times of
crisis, she may actually "carry"* part of his load: her cold
or headache may be a somatic mechanism for draining
the boss's hostility from her husband. Witness ex-Secretary of Defense McNamara's statement about his wife
when he resigned: "She has my ulcer."

During critical periods of danger, women rightfully
carried loads for their mates. No Neanderthal man could
successfully have staved off a saber-toothed tiger, thus

---

* The phenomenon of "loading" is a very interesting one which has
not been widely recognized nor had much scientific examination. It
first became apparent in intensive psychotherapy with character disorders, especially analysis potentiated by the use of certain inhibition-
lowering drugs. It was first observed (actually "felt" by members of
research group) immediately after a successful psychotherapy session
with a borderline patient who had had an intramuscular injection of
ritalin. The therapists and four aides present during the session experienced strong and almost identical feelings of being under pressure
and of unaccountable pains (back and right arm).

As the phenomenon was observed more often (it became completely
routine with subsequent work with the initial patient and others of
varying categories), it appeared as though the pathology of the illness —
the "burdens" of the illness — when dislodged, are taken up and
"carried" by those present at the session, much as packages too heavy
for one person to carry are distributed among other individuals.

The burdens of pressure, heaviness, aches and pains became so much
a routine part of drug-potentiated therapy that it became necessary
to develop techniques to discharge these loads: massage, strong physical
action such as rock and roll or rhythmic dancing, hot baths, stretch-
ings, and the one drug which seems specifically to relieve these particular pains — empirin and codein. Much needs to be examined and
understood about this process of load carrying since research group
members have been increasingly able to pinpoint its presence in everyday life. It seems to be involved in many seemingly intractable emotional problems and much psychosomatic illness. (Cf. B. G. Eisner,
"Psychedelics and People as Adjuncts to Psychotherapy," *British Journal of Social Psychiatry*, in press.)

insuring survival for himself and his family, with a bad head cold (or disturbed feelings which might have clouded his perception or betrayed the motor reflexes of his weapon arm) any more than he could go out and kill game with the hiccups. Just as Mrs. McNamara's ulcer enabled ex-Secretary McNamara to function more efficiently at his tension-producing job, a wife's migraine headache may have siphoned off her husband's hostility so that he can function smoothly at his work.

In caveman days this carrying of the emotional burden of physical disability for the necessarily active member of the team by the more passive member (children can develop into great load-carriers if the mother doesn't perform her job adequately and difficulties funnel off onto them) served a critical function for preservation of the family and for racial survival. However, today the situation is quite different: physical action is a small part of man's successful repertoire and is only valuable in cases of emergency or unusual stress; today it is mainly tension, anxiety, frustration, and inadequacy which a wife "manages" for her husband. This can have a beneficial result when the wife carries the emotional component of a specific difficulty for her husband, such as pressure from the boss or trouble with a fellow employee. Her sharing of his burden can make him feel better and her more adequate.

However, there is all too seldom a correlation between the illnesses and upsets which the wife carries and the amount of benefit her husband receives. No matter how hard she tries, the international threat grows, automation spreads and world tensions increase. Her husband doesn't feel any better because of her effort, and nothing meaningful seems to have been accomplished.

The carrying of loads when there is no apparent result, and no correlation between burden and relief, also joggles the cause-effect mechanism out of synchrony so that even a specialist — physician or therapist — is unable to track down the origin of the problem in order to deal with it.

Incidentally, it is interesting to note that individuals carry loads in different ways — each in his or her own unique fashion. The "difficulty" is probably "accepted" at a vulnerable spot. Sometimes a load carried on one person's body will be carried in exactly the same place by another person; at other times the load will be manifested differently. It appears as though there are certain areas of the body which are particularly subject to basic problems of hostility and inadequacy, and a load of any kind can have strength or pain enough to make it a real "headache" or "pain in the neck." Load carrying was probably one of the first forms and root beginnings of psychosomatic illness.

Women through the ages have been load carriers; their sense of adequacy and the race's survival depended on how well they managed to keep their mates operational without swamping themselves. Today, as we have seen, direct relationships rarely prevail, and there is instead disruption of the cause-effect mechanism, non-learning for the husband, and an unnecessarily heavy burden of pain for the wife without the relieving knowledge that she is helping her husband cope in a difficult world. How painful for a woman today — at a deep unconscious level and maybe even in actual awareness — to do her job without providing relief for her husband or experiencing a feeling of adequacy for herself.

Sometimes, and with increasing frequency nowadays, the roles are reversed, and a passive, dependent man is constantly ill — upset stomach, ulcers, psoriasis, or other psychosomatic ailments — from the loads he carries for his aggressive, dominating and unfeeling — in the sense of not being in tune with other people — wife. However, no matter which way the load has been shifted from its source, all burdens must be returned to their origin if they are to be understood, unraveled, and either integrated or disposed of. The original disability can be traced to its source through pain which can be used creatively to find the area and also provide the motive power for change. For mental health, all projections — and load carrying is a projection which results in a physical symptom — must be returned to their origins so that the process of cause and effect can work not only to demonstrate to the individual the consequences of his actions but also to give him information so that he can take responsibility for his actions and move toward changing the noncreative and destructive ones.

Consequences of Shifting Patterns

Because of the shift in roles for both men and women, and where the shift has brought diminishing satisfaction and lack of rewards in place of former dividends in adequacy and fulfillment, both men and women in modern society suffer acutely from feelings of worthlessness. Feelings of inadequacy multiply like hydra-headed monsters as individual human effort results less and less in a change of circumstances which will bring about a more peaceful and meaningful life.

The feelings of inadequacy which grow with a lack of connection between cause-and-effect and between action-

and-reward haunt modern man and his civilization like a specter at the banquet. Inadequacy grows on insecurity and ignorance of cause and effect; it feeds on any unfilled gap between potential and achievement and between fact and fantasy; and it waxes fat and poisonous on unfulfilled commitments and plans not translated into action.

Shifts in the equilibrium between men and women and changes in their roles with respect to each other and to themselves also contribute to feelings of inadequacy unless the individual can recognize the changes and accommodate to them.

Change always arouses anxiety and feelings of doubt as to how to understand and encompass the new. Since with each passing year the rate of change accelerates and the specific degree diminishes to which an individual can affect or modify elements of his own environment, is it any wonder that modern man feels helpless and at the mercy of forces beyond his control? One is reminded here of the theatre of the absurd: of Beckett's *Waiting for Godot*, in which the characters wait endlessly for someone who is going to do some unspecified thing to help them; or Kafka's *The Trial*, in which the hero finds himself on trial for an unknown crime without the possibility of seeing his accusers or being able to answer the unspecified charges.

One of the most critical areas of breakdown of known patterns of behavior without the substitution of new guidelines has been in the sexual realm. The resulting turmoil has produced stress throughout society, particularly in two areas: in widening the generation gap; and in adding further, almost intolerable, stress and strain to the relationship between men and women, particularly marriage partners.

When a man — or woman — feels an inadequacy or a lack, he has two courses of action: he can attempt to escape the pain of the gap, fleeing into passivity with alcohol, drugs, television, or into activity with compulsive work or play; or he can move to fill it. If he is perceptive and knowledgeable about himself, he will discover the nature of the lack and act in such a manner as to take care of it. If he is neurotic, he will move blindly toward anything which will create an equilibrium and make him feel better — usually a relationship which he can hope to make permanent. Thus, men and women, plagued by anxiety about the future and their frustration from not being able to manage meaningful responses, leap into each other's arms in interlocking dependencies, seeking everything from psychological adequacy to cosmic meaning in a one-to-one relationship with another human being.

When compulsive action to avoid inadequacy feelings results in marriage, difficulties multiply. After the first flush of the honeymoon is over, what initially were single immaturities and frustrations become compounded into interlocking double binds between husband and wife. These fusions or intermeshings serve to create an equilibrium — although a neurotic one — because the relationship is immobilized against movement, and each individual's potential and the potential of the relationship are prematurely limited.

Immobilization protects an individual against change, and it also inhibits growth. The interlocking neurosis resulting from the "marriage" of two neurotic individuals is one of the main resistance-forces which works to prevent individuals from maturing so that they can creatively meet the challenges of life and move along the path toward fulfilling their potential.

The phenomenon of interlocking neurosis is so important that it warrants consideration at some length.

3

Destructive Duet
—the Interlocking Neurosis

IN any neurotic relationship between two people
there are three neuroses: the neurosis of each of the
individuals involved, and the interlocking neurosis. For
example, in marriage these might be called his, hers, and
theirs.

Recognition of this third, previously unsuspected neurosis has been gradually emerging into view. Psychotherapy is one of the better vantage points for observation of
the phenomenon, provided it is deep psychotherapy which
attempts change of the character of the individuals, and
provided the same therapist works with both partners of
a marriage. The couple must be closely observed over a
considerable period of time in the process of acting as a
unit as well as two separate individuals. It is during the
observation of the intricate interactions between two
closely related people (who can be mother and child as
well as husband and wife) that the pattern emerges
clearly.

As observed, this third — or interlocking — neurosis is

the meshing and fusing together of the emotional difficulties, personality problems, and immaturities of the two individual neuroses; it is the pattern formed by the union of uncreative combinations operating between two people in close relationship.

It consists of a number of elements: complementary defensive systems (You bomb; I'll balm); dovetailing methods of expressing or controlling basic drives (from Peter, Peter, pumpkin eater, and his wife in the pumpkin shell to Jack Sprat, who ate only lean while his wife ate all the fat); sadomasochistic interactions, such as those of Martha and George in *Who's Afraid of Virginia Woolf* and the husband and wife in *The Shrike*; meshing mechanisms for filling dependencies, such as exemplified by Vladimir and Estragon in *Waiting for Godot* and by Baby Doll, whose husband kept her as a child, allowing her to suck her thumb and sleep in a crib and have no responsibilities; down to the rock-bottom interpenetrating inadequacies of symbiotic (parasite-host) fusion such as those seen between Trilby and Svengali, Pygmalion and Galatea, and the frequent examples of spouses who either die or commit suicide within a few weeks of the death of their mates.

With an interlocking neurosis it is as though an unspoken contract exists at the heart of the relationship: "You fill my lacks, I'll fill your lacks, and we'll both fight to the death to protect the status quo. Further, our narcissisms will be satisfied, our omnipotence will survive, and we will be *somebody* through total involvement with each other."

Neurosis consists of inefficient and outmoded habit patterns which in childhood served the purpose of emotional survival — the price in later life being a malfunctioning adult. Neurotic mechanisms have at their root a resistance to change. With an interlocking neurosis the process becomes a double bind to maintain the status quo and to remain wholly interconnected.

The strength of the commitment not to change becomes most apparent when one or both partners of a marriage enter therapy. As one personal neurosis begins to unravel and that individual begins to change, a disequilibrium is created, and an immediate stress is imposed on the relationship. This is interpreted as an attack by the static member, who — perceiving incorrectly that he or she has been fired upon — reacts strongly. The flags on the battlements of the interlocking neurosis go up; the bugle sounds charge, and the attacking defenses of the mate sally forth from the citadel. One army calls forth another, and suddenly the plain is brilliant with the multiplicity of maneuvers and tactics to distract energy and attention from the true battle — that of facing the issue at hand.

Or, rather than attacking, the partner who feels attacked may choose to run. Flight or fight always calls forth complementary reactions. This sets off the reverberating circuits of maneuvers oriented toward making a big production rather than solving the problem.

It appears that the operation of the interlocking neurosis has been much better delineated in literature and drama — even nursery rhymes — than in psychiatry. For example, what else but monumental fear, inadequacy, and flight from change would force Jim, after his suicide attempt in *The Shrike*, to choose his wife Anne, dedicated to his emasculation, in preference to the mental hospital

— even though he had just tried to kill himself because of his inability to escape from his dependency on her?

Early in that inspired picturization of interlocking neurosis, *Who's Afraid of Virginia Woolf*, Martha and George start into a bickering which later becomes a raging psychic life and death struggle.

MARTHA: Hey, put some more ice in my drink, will you? You never put any ice in my drink.

GEORGE: (*Takes her drink*) I always put ice in your drink. You eat it, that's all. It's that habit you have . . . chewing your ice cubes . . . like a cocker spaniel. You'll crack your big teeth.

MARTHA: THEY'RE MY BIG TEETH!

GEORGE: Some of them . . . some of them.

MARTHA: I've got more teeth than you've got.

GEORGE: Two more.

MARTHA: Well, two more's a lot.

GEORGE: I suppose it is. I suppose it's pretty remarkable . . . considering how old you are.

MARTHA: YOU CUT THAT OUT. (*Pause*) You're not so young yourself.

GEORGE: (*With boyish pleasure . . . a chant*) I'm six years younger than you are . . . I always have been and I always will be.

MARTHA: (*Glumly*) Well . . . you're going bald.

GEORGE: So are you. (*Pause . . . they both laugh*) Hello, honey.

MARTHA: Hello. C'mon over here and give your mommy a big sloppy kiss.

GEORGE: . . . oh . . . now . . .

MARTHA: I WANT A BIG SLOPPY KISS!

GEORGE: (*Preoccupied*) I don't *want* to kiss you, Martha. Where *are* those people? Where are those *people* you invited over?

When Martha had married, she and her father thought George was an up-and-coming member of the history department destined to follow in her father's footsteps, but since then she had seen a combination of factors — mainly her father — destroy her husband's attempts at success. She drinks too much and is promiscuous, continually trying to obliterate the fact that she feels inadequate as a woman.

Her husband, George, feels inadequate as a man because his success has not been up to his potential, and he certainly has not succeeded as his wife and his father-in-law think he should have. The play unravels its length before the audience finds out that Martha's great inadequacy as a woman stems in part from her inability to have a child — such an agonizing inability that she creates a fantasy son. George goes along with this illusion of hers when they are together; he will even allow its use discriminatingly with others — or until Martha launches some lethal attack on him.

George's inadequacy as a man with respect to his career (and as the having-been-designated-heir-apparent-who-didn't-make-it) interlocks with Martha's inadequacy as a woman in her incapacity to have a child. They protect these lacks in each other as long as neither pushes the other too hard.

Besides overt bickering and warfare, a more subtle pattern of the interlocking neurosis is alternating self-defeating action: when one member of the couple is functioning well, the other must be sick and helpless. Consider *Two for the Seesaw*, where Gittel could take care of Gerry as long as he was broke and without a job; once he had part-time work and was studying for his successful bar examination, she cultivated an ulcer flare-up into several months of complete invalidism.

This neurotic seesaw interaction is very familiar to us in everyday life: when one spouse is "up" the other is correspondingly "down" — an oscillation which applies in everything from physical health and emotional conditions to everyday mood swings. It is particularly lethal in that most delicate of human interactions, lovemaking — when as one partner is warm and willing, the other is indifferent and withdrawn.

A variation of the seesaw is the "minuet of rejection," whereby as one member of the couple approaches, the other retreats until the pursuer gets discouraged; then the roles shift and pursuer immediately becomes pursued. This approach-avoidance mechanism reminds one of electromagnetic attraction, which at a certain point shifts poles so that the attraction becomes repulsion. It is a common means of approaching or learning about a new situation; however, it is a very dangerous dance to be engaged in after a pair know each other and can become a macabre sword dance and destroy possibilities of continuing openness between the couple.

Another neurotic pattern of interlocking action involves two forms of resonance: one is the stirring up of emotions in the other person in order to create conditions for a guilt-free fight; the other mechanism occurs when one feels an emotion that is uncomfortable and manages things in such a way that the partner expresses the uncomfortable emotion.

All of us have observed how a tired husband, full of the hostility he was unable to express at work, takes it out on his wife and children. The wife, if she is unable to understand and accept the tirade, bickers back or flares into fiery attack.

With the second mechanism, which works like physical resonance, the husband starts expressing his anger. As he proceeds, his wife's emotional temperature begins to rise and she gets increasingly angry. Finally the husband is peacefully content, anger gone, and she is furious at his boss, or at the world in general. Similarly, a hard-fought PTA meeting can be worked out by way of a husband's increasing ire.

This reverberating resonance must be differentiated from load carrying, which occurs when one individual takes over the burden of another as his own. Load carrying is a common aspect of all forms and levels of relationship and, as we have discussed, probably had its inception back in caveman days in the service of survival of the race. It is a very important aspect of relationship, and its spectrum ranges from creative load carrying, in which the burden one member of a pair takes on for the other is actually valuable or fun for him to assume, to a sadomasochistic relationship, in which one of the partners, either husband or wife, carries all of the negative qualities and action-consequences of the other, even to the extreme of emotional breakdown, physical breakdown, or death.

The whole interesting concept of load carrying is, psychologically speaking, relatively unmapped territory. Women are notorious load carriers: historically, as part of their role; psychologically, because according to the laws of emotional gravity burdens are displaced downward through hierarchical patterns of drainage. This is called pecking order when it becomes more of a hostility discharge than burden dispensing. It is very common to see families in which one of the children has become the load carrier or the psychic garbage disposal for the whole family. A child so trained to accept the negative aspects of the rest of the family is beautifully conditioned for the receiving end of a sadomasochistic marriage relationship. Or, if the child's psyche is not strong enough to stand the strain, he is being prepared for time in a mental institution.

Family psychotherapy, the relatively new practice of dealing with the emotional problems of a very disturbed child by treating the whole family together (the practice of solving pathological relationship problems within the family circle with all members present and working therapeutically) has revealed dramatic cases where one member of the family was the scapegoat for problems of one or more other members of the family. Family therapy, incidentally, appears to be one of the fastest ways out of the multi-determined interlocking binds, just as conjoint therapy works better for a couple (both together) than individual therapy.

Psychotherapy in general has been very inept about solving the problem of the interlocking neurosis: usually there is no clear picture — often, in fact, there is no clear concept — of what is operating in this double bind against change. Psychoanalysis has been peculiarly inept because of its ritual whereby no two marriage partners may see the same analyst. This is almost a guarantee of divorce during the course of therapy, if therapy is to be "successful" at all.*

---

* Statistics are hard to come by, probably because of the understandable reticence of therapists. My experience and that of colleagues (obtained by informal survey) indicates that more than half the marriages in which one partner enters psychoanalysis end in dissolution. If the partner undertakes intensive psychotherapy with a psychiatrist, the figure is around 25 percent; if marital counseling (whether with a psychiatrist, psychologist or social worker), about 10 percent. When both partners are seen together by the therapist, there is a much smaller percentage of dissolution.

"Marriage counselors who have a high rate of success in rejoining so-called 'broken homes' have told me that, in their practical, actual experience, psychoanalysis does more to defeat marriage than the original, seemingly intolerable situation which initiated the conjugal dissolution . . .

"Only one woman out of the several hundred I have talked with regarding psychoanalysis and divorces told me her analyst insisted on her staying married. She also added that her analyst reached this decision after questioning her as to the source of her income" (her husband's money was necessary for her therapy). (E. R. Pinckney and C. Pinckney, *The Fallacy of Freud and Psychoanalysis*, New York, Prentice-Hall, 1965, ch. 7.)

Dr. Nathan Hurvitz ("Marital Problems Following Psychotherapy with One Spouse," *Journal of Consulting Psychology*, vol. 31, 1969, pp. 38–47) says, "Greater marital discord after therapy with one spouse appears so often that it may be inherent in such relationships. . . . The therapy disturbs the relationship between the spouses, old difficulties and problems are complicated and intensified, new problems are created, and their marriage may be destroyed. Both spouses may then be referred to a marriage counselor for help. . . ."

Dr. Monica J. Blumenthal, in an excellent study ("Mental Health Among the Divorced," *Archives of General Psychiatry*, vol. 16, 1967, pp. 603–608), found a significant difference in the mental health of divorced and nondivorced individuals: "Divorced persons show more mental illness as measured by our mental health indices than people who never divorced" (that is, more mental hospital admissions, higher crime and alcoholism rate, poorer adjustment to people and jobs).

It is interesting that all statistics show that divorce increases significantly with decreasing social class.

In the case of well-entrenched emotional illness (particularly with character disorders), when the patient's personal neurosis starts to unravel, the defenses of the interlocking neurosis come into violent activation. Defenses are aroused because of the inordinate mutual demands which arise from the strength of the fused-together symbiotic† relationship and the interlocking of omnipotence-inadequacy-identity factors. The emotional feelings of the participants are like that of parasite and host. There is no possibility of survival for the parasite without the host, and both individuals play both roles. It is like an illusory, encapsulated world where both partners simultaneously feel all-powerful and at the same time completely taken care of. Narcissism is satisfied by the totality of neurotic involvement, and any deficits of identity, such as diffusion or displacement, are obscured by the mechanism of the interlock.

The forces aroused by a threat to this relationship of interlocking necessity are explosive: the couple's psyches crash together with such violence and hostility that they sometimes have to be separated physically at this time in order to prevent serious injury. Or they may fly so far apart that no amount of time, work, or good will can bridge the chasm.

Interlocking neuroses are particularly tough and impenetrable in neurotic marriages where creative levels and positive qualities are also interwoven and fused. We have found that those individuals who are very strongly drawn together as much for creative reasons as for nega-

---

† Symbiotic fusion is a completely interdependent state of co-existence such as parasite and host where both members of the symbiosis play both roles for each other, being both parasite and host.

tive ones, and who really ultimately "belong" together as a couple, have the greatest difficulty in separating the growth elements from the neurotic ones. Just as the finer the meshing between gears, the greater the difficulty in freeing from each other without damage a pair which has been frozen together.

Besides the fusion of attraction, and the fusions of defensiveness and inadequacy, the most intricately meshed couples appear to have a mutual transference of the whole childhood situation onto each other. In marriage, one tends to attempt to re-create early childhood situations — but in a manner in which they can be solved. Sometimes the "solution" is merely a re-creation of an insecure family situation within the "indissoluble" bond of marriage so that "rejection" is impossible; sometimes the "solution" is the old family homestead with the once dominated child now in authoritarian control; sometimes the re-creation is in the service of working toward a more creative solution. In any case, early family figures or combinations of figures (as projected onto someone) are sought out as marriage partners.

With intricate and complicated people, and in very neurotic combinations, it is as though two families have married each other rather than two individuals. In these marriages, the couple can play every role for each other, or all sorts of combinations of roles. When in the course of psychotherapy and working through problems with mother, the interlocking neurosis kicks up as the mother transference is activated; when father appears on the scene, there is again a fierce turbulence; and when it comes to sibling interactions, the cauldron comes to a violent boil.

Actually, the problems with the siblings repeat those with the parents with additions: competitive reactions are heightened because the actual struggle in the past was most often with siblings; companionship-mating relationships are intensified with displacement of unresolved oedipal feelings from the parents down the generation gap to the siblings who are in the appropriate age group.

The true loyalty in a family should be among the siblings; if there is any forsaking all for each other, it is the brothers and sisters who should desert mother, father, uncles, aunts, and all the rest of the family in order to create an operational bond to each other. If the growing child is unable to "forsake" the adult entanglements as he matures and works out his feelings of inadequacy, narcissism, and omnipotence with his age group, he will have a great deal of trouble forsaking all other commitments for the one commitment to a marriage partner. Of course the primary problems arise with mother, then extend to father. However, the resolution can only proceed to a certain point with parents; the real working through must occur with one's peers — or siblings — or in actuality it usually occurs with the marriage partner.

It appears to be a far better guarantee of growing up to psychological maturity to have a good relationship with a number of siblings than with one or both parents. Harlow's monkeys come to mind here: monkeys deprived of a mother could survive to normally operating adulthood with a cloth mother provided they were brought up with other young monkeys; however, young monkeys deprived of siblings did not grow up to normal adulthood even though they had flesh and blood mothers.

If in the course of growing up the child defects from

his siblings — especially to join the adults — he is afflicted by guilt much greater than any guilt felt through defection from either or both parents. Witness the strength of bonds between "brothers" such as David and Jonathan, Siegmund and Sieglinde, the countless examples of families of children sticking together after parents have died, and of older brothers and sisters raising and educating younger siblings. Compare this to the hatred and scorn (and his guilt) felt toward someone like Judas who betrayed not only Jesus but all twelve of his brothers. Even those siblings who draw away from their brothers and sisters in achievement (money, fame, activities) often carry strange feelings of vague guilt at having surpassed the rest of the family.

There seems to be some sort of necessary imperative which demands that the primary loyalty of the members of each generation be to each other — probably to maintain creative growth conditions and unity for their own continuing relationships.

A further problem with interlocking neurosis is time. Time, besides locking in the past through the conditioning of early experience and environment, also biases the future through illusory expectations — whether from over-grandiosity or from the "loser" (I can't win no matter what I do) syndrome. Time complicates an interlocking neurosis further by introducing false timelessness: marriages are supposedly made in heaven — forever. Even though divorce is accepted and occurs so widely, we are not more than half a century from the time when parting was unthinkable socially and many churches (especially the Catholic) still make it virtually impossible for an individual to marry another partner after rupturing from the first one. Despite the divorce rate, people in the United States feel in some part of their emotions that marriage is "until death us do part," and consequently there is a great deal of guilt along with feelings of failure when marriages break up.

Because of the emotional expectation of "forever" in marriage, the agreement to protect each other's neurotic limitations and inadequacies gains an aura of eternity. Thus, any fight, no matter how small the initial issue, has the possibility of becoming a battle of "forever" proportions.

The most spectacular and lethal fights (or actions) occur when one of the partners intrudes into the central core of the inadequacy of his mate, the inadequacy which lies at the center of any neurosis. It is the pain of feelings of total helplessness and inadequacy and the necessity to protect this area of agony which give rise to interlocking dependencies and symbiotic (parasite-host) fusion. The two participants in an interlocking neurosis find in each other meshing areas of inadequacy feelings which can be mutually defended against intrusion from outside forces.

The feeling of being totally helpless in the face of a difficult if not outright hostile environment is one which is common to all human beings; the experiencing of it is avoided universally because it is so painful. If there have been traumatic emotional experiences in early childhood, the feeling of helplessness at the core is made further hideous by perceiving the world not only as passively hostile but also as lethally active in an attempt to destroy.

It is like death or insanity to feel the tearing away of reality as we know it — reality and the illusions of how we think we are — and to be plunged into the quicksands of our own inadequacies. When this occurs one disintegrates into a helpless, quivering mass of protoplasm.

The agony of this encounter with inadequacy is so great that individuals flee headlong into frying pan, fire, death, and psychosis in order to escape its terrible confrontation. The greater the inadequacy a person feels, the greater the neurotic convolutions that have been developed to avoid its pain. Further, the more numerous and severe the resulting neurotic mechanisms, the less likelihood there is of shifting inadequacy into fulfilled capacity because neurosis, by its very nature, obscures the operation of cause-and-effect. The direct cause-and-effect relationships from the experience of completion and achievement are required in order to drain the unconscious storehouse of inadequacy.

Two beautiful examples in literature of individuals pushed to the encounter with their inadequacies are Willy Loman in *Death of a Salesman* and Hamlet.

Hamlet, in the following soliloquy, speaks about his feelings when events have pushed him to desperation arising from his incapacity to act as he feels he should to avenge the murder of his father.

O, what a rogue and peasant slave am I! . . .
A dull and muddy-mettled rascal, peak,
Like John-a-dreams, unpregnant of my cause,
And I can say nothing . . .
Am I a coward?
Who calls me villain? breaks my pate across?
Tweaks me by the nose? gives me the lie i' the throat,
As deep as to the lungs? who does this?

Ha!
Swounds, I should take it: for it cannot be
But I am pigeon-liver'd and lack gall
To make oppression bitter . . .
Why, what an ass am I! This is most brave,
That I, the son of a dear father murder'd
Prompted to my revenge by heaven and hell,
Must, like a whore, unpack my heart with words,
And fall a-cursing, like a very drab,
A scullion!

Arthur Miller in *Death of a Salesman* shows the dis-integration of Willy Loman as his illusions are torn away and as he is forced deeper and deeper into his failure and inadequacy — until the only way out for him is suicide. The portrait of a man heading lethally into his own help-less, hopeless inadequacy is displayed when the curtain rises on the first act:

LINDA: (*Hearing Willy outside the bedroom, calls with trepidation*) Willy!

WILLY: It's all right. I came back.

LINDA: Why? What happened? (*Slight pause*) Did something happen, Willy?

WILLY: No, nothing happened.

LINDA: You didn't smash the car, did you?

WILLY: (*With casual irritation*) I said nothing hap-pened. Didn't you hear me?

LINDA: Don't you feel well?

WILLY: I'm tired to death. (*The flute has faded away. He sits on the bed beside her, a little numb.*) I couldn't make it. I just couldn't make it, Linda.

[37]

LINDA: (*Very carefully, delicately*) Where were you all day? You look terrible.

WILLY: I got as far as a little above Yonkers. I stopped for a cup of coffee. Maybe it was the coffee.

LINDA: What?

WILLY: (*After a pause*) I suddenly couldn't drive any more. The car kept going off onto the shoulder, y'know?

LINDA: (*Helpfully*) Oh. Maybe it was the steering again. I don't think Angelo knows the Studebaker.

WILLY: No, it's me, it's me. Suddenly I realize I'm going sixty miles an hour, and I don't remember the last five minutes. I'm — I can't seem to — keep my mind to it.

LINDA: Maybe it's your glasses. You never went for your new glasses.

WILLY: No, I see everything. I came back ten miles an hour. It took me nearly four hours from Yonkers.

LINDA: (*Resigned*) Well, you'll just have to take a rest, Willy. You can't continue this way.

WILLY: I just got back from Florida.

LINDA: But you didn't rest your mind. Your mind is overactive, and the mind is what counts, dear.

It is only after long and arduous application — and where the commitment to change and growth has become greater than the commitment to neurosis and status quo — that the defenses begin to diminish and probes are allowed into that area of agony — of basic inadequacy and lack of identity. It is at this time, when the commitment to health is greater than the commitment to neurosis, that the partner allows the spouse to change for the better — no matter the consequences in neurotic pain to himself.

In an interlocking neurosis, the central area is declared off limits by the contract guaranteeing the status quo. In fact, it is at this site that the symbiotic (parasite-host) fusion takes place: convex inadequacies attract and fuse with concave ones; the active man finds a passive woman (or vice versa); the sadist meets his complementary masochist; the explosive personality locates a damping one and opposites meet and mesh. Here the topography of character and personality dovetail so beautifully that there is almost automatic protection of the central area.

Access to this area is mutually off limits by neurotic agreement, whether because of early experiences in common or overlapping character patterns. Where these mutual agreements are respected, the relationship lasts. However, if there is *too* much interaction in the areas of each other's pain, the relationships are transient, rarely leading to marriage because of the violence of the conflicts engendered by the continuous pushing of panic-inadequacy buttons. Examples of the tragedies which can occur when such relationships do happen to be solidified make headlines as, for instance, an estranged husband killing his wife and anyone else who happens to be with her at the time.

A valuable barometer of the neurotic forces in a marriage is the lack of compunction — or actual willingness — of husband or wife to push each other's master switch. And while the interaction between husband and wife in this area may look like sadomasochism, it is only secondarily so. The primary force is the interlocking of the dependency which lies deep in the taproot of inadequacy, together with the unerring knowledge each member has concerning the other's specific vulnerability.

[39]

Just as Martha in *Who's Afraid of Virginia Woolf* knew that her husband, George, could not tolerate any mention of his failure to become head of the history department, so also George knew that Martha could not be without her fantasied son — the son who gave her, in her own and other's eyes, the status of motherhood.

They knew the exact spot and the exact sharpness of the weapon* of intrusion required to inflict maximum hurt on each other. It is as though, along with the contract to defend each other's inadequacies to the death, access is given to the vital spot of sensitivity. Of course, a gentlemen's agreement prevails, and only in moments of stress — one's own stress, of course — is it permitted to touch this spot. However, the button can be toyed with, and it becomes an added neurotic game to see how close one can come to putting force on the other's panic button and still carry on an act of complete innocence.

But let anyone else intrude into the sacred area of the master switch and immediately both individuals are up in arms. Each member of an encapsulated neurotic relationship defends his right to be the sole intruder into his mate's lack of identity. For example, when Nick, the young biology professor in *Virginia Woolf*, brings up the hideous fact that George accidentally killed both his mother and father in young adulthood, Martha and

---

* Recent studies illustrate the extreme sensitivity existing between two individuals who are emotionally close. Dr. G. E. Rice of Montana State University found that mothers showed a galvanic skin response when their daughters heard a shot, as did wives when their husbands stepped into a tub of ice water. Dr. Aristide H. Esser found at Rockland State Hospital, New York, that the alpha waves of identical twins are synchronized and a wife in another room registers the same changed anatomical response (heart rate, pressure, brain waves) as her husband when shown the picture of his beautiful ex-fiancée.

George immediately drop their fight with each other, swing on Nick, and attack him simultaneously.

But what of an interlocked couple? Can the concept of the interlocking neurosis help them? Does it help the couple to know that there is a third complicating factor — their interaction — in addition to their own two individual problems? Does this enable them to live together with more satisfaction and fulfillment?

Perhaps the knowledge by itself won't do them much good. However, knowledge does make available a wider range of choices. Alternative courses of action — such as choice among varying types of therapy — are made possible. Also, the examination of the anatomy of the process of interpenetrating emotional problems may provide insights into their relationship and behavior with one another. At least they will have some indication of the direction in which they must move; or, if they don't have the energy or motivation to move, then the implications of inaction can be examined.

It is not an easy task to change not only one person, but two — plus their interaction. It takes a great deal of time and energy, and is paid for only incidentally with money. The real payment is in pain — the peeled-off skin and the knife-in-the-gut pain of basic change.

But is existence in the interlocking neurosis any easier? Martha has a very touching scene with Nick where she reveals her feelings about her relationship with George. She seems helpless and hopeless. Is this a state to be cherished?

MARTHA: George, who is out somewhere in the dark ... George, who is good to me, and whom I revile; who understands me, and whom I push off; who can hold me, at night, so that it's warm, and whom I will bite so there's blood; who keeps learning the games we play as quickly as I can change the rules; who can make me happy and I do not wish to be happy. George and Martha: sad, sad, sad.

NICK: (*echoing, still not believing*) Sad . . .

When the neurotic contract is a strongly binding one, possessiveness is obviously a concomitant. The better the defensive meshing and the more levels at which there is fusion, the greater the need of the two partners for each other. This forms mutual dependency. When dependency appears hostility is right behind, and possessiveness is born of their union. The couple need each other in order to avoid feeling their own inadequacy and lack of identity.

It is almost as though modern man acts out of the compulsive necessity to avoid both inadequacy feelings and awareness of lack of identity, thus becoming dependent on his methods of avoidance. At least there is something to be done about feelings of inadequacy if one is able to face the problem squarely and if one is willing to grow past the area of limitation. This is not true with dependency which is always camouflaged in vestments other than its own.

Most commonly, dependency is hidden under a camouflage of hostility: the more Esmerelda needs Jebediah, the more hostile she becomes. When dependency is combined with unconscious needs to fail or to be punished, the individual makes it impossible to have his needs fulfilled, thus increasing the amount of hostility. For instance, when Esmerelda has had a difficult day and wants Jebediah to come home and take her in his arms (needing badly his sympathy) her dependency (unacceptable to herself and dooming her to failure by its combination with feelings that she can never win) causes her to work up a good case of anger at Jebediah before he even arrives. As a result she may greet him at the door with a blast of anger, or palpable sulkiness, thus guaranteeing to put him into a mood which makes it impossible for him to give her the solace she so badly needs. Just as the Irishman, badly needing a sleigh and walking through the snow to borrow his neighbor's, so worked himself up over the thought that he might not be able to have it that he greeted the owner as his door opened, "Well now, and you can keep your god-damned sleigh!"

Possessiveness is the frontier post of dependency. Sometimes it is very pronounced, straightforward, and precise, which makes it easier to deal with. Harry makes it very clear that he doesn't want Lulubelle to look at another man — let alone dance with one — or even have coffee during breaks with any other than female companionship, that is, if his possessiveness allows Lulubelle to work outside of the home. Lulubelle, if possessive, clings to her husband, is violently jealous of any female co-worker, and creates a scene whenever the poor man turns his head to look at a bikini.

Mostly, however, the hostility that masks dependency is covert or unconscious. After all, if we show anger or even acknowledge that it is there we threaten our security because the one we need may reject us. So the hostility is hidden and Zorba may verbally give his wife freedom to go anywhere with anyone she likes. However, should

Josephine try to take advantage of this liberalness, she may find that the days she has planned to go out there is no car available; subtle remarks are made about her friends, even her closest women friends; and any real endeavor on her part to reach out to a larger life is blocked by seemingly meaningless coincidences or subtle variations of Zorba's moods.

The husband or wife who is violently jealous and possessive but overreacts on the surface with seemingly cooperative tolerance will displace the problem into peripheral areas. Hostility will be directed toward matters of dress, or personal habits and choice of activities become scenes of major battles. What possible forward motion in relationship can be resolved with a violent fight over the color of lipstick or the length of a dress when it merely represents a husband's fear of a friend — even a woman friend — coming between his wife and himself? What resolution of a wife's nagging-to-explosion of her husband for using a knife as well as a fork to cut his salad can help when it was really her discomfort with her husband's friendliness toward another woman that was really bothering her?

Further (and even more diabolically destructive to relationship), once an interlocking neurosis is established, the neurotic goal becomes control of the other partner. This control is felt, usually unconsciously, to be vitally necessary: it must be maintained to insure that there will be no loss of the other half of the combination with all the attendant pain and desolation; and to ensure that neurotic needs are met with minimal expenditure of energy (on the part of the one controlling) and without impingement on possible sensitive areas.

Of course the neurotic needs may be that the wife is beaten every other day — otherwise she is subject to agonizing guilt and he is full of explosive hostility; or that the husband suffer through an endless procession of affairs — either his own or his wife's; or that either husband or wife be a martyr at whatever activity the couple jointly, although unconsciously, decide. The satisfaction of neurotic needs may bear no resemblance to the satisfaction of true needs for fulfillment or for creative living. However, dependency needs can mimic legitimate needs, creating the appearance of growth or managing to camouflage flight from the pain of change into pseudo-health or into apparent creativity.

This neurotic control is exerted in all the myriad ways available to an inventive human being (words, expressions, actions, emotions, the repertoire of behavior) in order to guarantee the desired (secure) response from the partner.

One of the most common and effective control mechanisms is the manipulation of guilt (cf. a good Yiddisher momma). This is a subtle game whose basic rules are absorbed by the child along with his mother's milk and whose goal is to keep the other member of the team just guilty enough so that he or she will do the manipulator's bidding, even if they have to be seduced into hitting the manipulator every once in a while in order to manage this.

Children from difficult backgrounds — difficult in the sense that they were mistaught cause-and-effect in behavior and were made to feel at fault for things beyond their control — early develop masterful defense mechanisms against the imposition of guilt. These individuals sense guilt — whether legitimate or not — acutely well, and they turn the guilt back on the one attempting to impose it — sometimes directly and sometimes so subtly that the interchange is almost impossible to detect.

With interlocking neurosis the individuals have chosen their partners well: no matter what the imposed guilt may appear to be, it is felt for what it is, and the receiver reacts to it in his own special style. It becomes rather like a complicated game of tennis, but with the added requirement that both sides must, as they play the game, pretend that there is no tennis ball flying back and forth — in fact, they must even pretend that no game is in progress.

However, this is not just a game of seeing who can return the ball the longer or score the most points; underneath, it is a deadly serious control ploy whose goal is to insure that the other member of the relationship will be kept one down just enough so that there will be no disturbance of the status quo. The relationship must be maintained at all times within the limits of the proper distance from each other's master switch of inadequacy-panic and for the assurance of uninterrupted dependency.

Another control mechanism is the bargain — both overt and implied. Overtly it goes: "You let me have that new dress that I want, and I'll not make a fuss when you want to play golf the weekend my family is here." Or, "I'll take care of the children for you tonight if I can have that extra night with the bowling league." Covertly: the wife cooks an especially nice dinner for her husband when she wants to ask him for something.

Even more subtle is: "Let's goof off together and then we'll let each other off the hook." For example: "Let's watch television and have that long overdue evening together," says Jeannette to Pablo when he comes home for dinner. Pablo leaps at the suggestion, conveniently overlooking the fact that he had committed himself to finishing up the income tax returns that night, maybe after having proclaimed his intention loudly ever since there had not been time on the "overcrowded" weekend. At the same time Pablo may have forgotten — or he may never have known — that Jeannette had promised a book review for the PTA the next day, and a survey of her recipe file for the school collection — neither of which could be completed if she didn't work that night.

You goof off, and *I'll* goof off, and we won't tell anyone and neither of us will feel guilty because we'll both be in the same goof boat! Lovely mechanism, until the dawn of cause-and-effect breaks, and both participants find themselves at the end of the race without having left the starting line.

There is a subtle one-up variation of this game, which is actually a lethal ploy on manipulation of guilt. One of the members of the goof-off contract at the last moment pulls out of the agreement. Having involved the spouse to the point where he or she can't extricate themselves — deep in an exciting TV show or all dressed up to go out to dinner or the movies — he (or she) one-ups the partner by withdrawing from the goofing off and setting to on the work which needs to be done. This leaves one "good" member, one "bad" member, a bunch of seething hostility (intensified by innocent smugness), and guilt first over nonaccomplishment and secondly over the hostility — all of which guilt is then subject to further manipulation.

In order to pull off ploys of this subtlety and effectiveness (genius?), one must be a master in the art of manipulating time. Used neurotically, but gently, it can be nothing more than a valuable and slightly nasty game for one or both members of the interlocking neurosis where the variations are so infinite and so complicated that it takes a genius to catch a master. It can also be a lethal weapon to drive someone to insanity — or murder. Witness the effect of the manipulations of time and other small shifts in the environment such as lights going on and off in the movie *Gaslight*; think of a word spoken too late which makes a reprieve impossible; and remember the macabre cartoon showing a Charles Addams character waving a car to pass his sports roadster around a mountain turn on whose other side a truck more than fills the lane.

With respect to the manipulation of time, there is procrastination and double procrastination and there is antiprocrastination — arriving early in order to make it appear as though the other member is late. There is arriving early and leaving early but getting home late. There are all sorts of possibilities, and this is just in such a simple matter as two people meeting each other. In fact, all of the intelligence — even genius — of an individual who is neurotically rather than creatively directed can go toward fabricating variations of these games and their use and timing so that it is impossible to put one's finger on what is being done and how. Given two opponents worthy of their neurotic metal and equally matched in intelligence and skill, the resulting impasse is impossible to assess, and relationship becomes a hopelessly complicated mass of compounded concrete.

Funny? Yes, when one sees Charlie Chaplin or Laurel

and Hardy entangled in its meshes; sometimes funny for oneself if not too serious a bind results and one is swept by a sudden moment of self-revelation. But mostly it is irritating, infuriating, and wasteful of time and efficiency. Sometimes it taps in on lethality and explosiveness — ending with the trips to insanity of *Gaslight* and *The Shrike* or the murder or suicide which follows when insane anger is driven beyond its bounds.

Pain is the inevitable by-product of the interlocking neurosis. Interlocking neurosis is a painful situation because it is a breach of the contract we all have with growth and with time. As living beings we are committed to life and to growth; as biological organisms we can move only in one direction in time — forward. We are not dead or lifeless like metals, for instance, and we cannot reverse ourselves; they can melt or harden as the situation dictates, moving backward or forward in time.

Nothing can halt the measured sequence of time for a biological organism; neurosis only gives the illusion of so doing. (Psychosis tries to maintain the illusion of being outside of time.) Also, nothing can prevent necessary and appropriate change without causing deep and possibly lasting damage to those who have the blindness or the delusions of grandeur great enough to attempt it. Since time moves only in one direction for us, there is the implicit commitment to change which is inherent in being a living organism. The double padlocks of the commitment against change implicit in the interlocking neurosis reverberate painfully much of the time in its participants.

But do the participants recognize this? Even if Esmerelda and Jebediah are doubled up in agony from their interactions, would it occur to them to stop a process which is so painful to them both?

No, probably not — even if they could. The very interaction satisfies needs. The interlocking neurosis gives each member the illusion not only of being someone who is totally involved, but also of having another individual totally involved with him. The narcissistic supplies may be trouble, toil, and pain, but they *are* supplies. If a third party suddenly offered the couple freedom from their "prison" both would shrink back into the security of the familiar cell or else would offer their "savior" a poke in the nose for interference and the failure to "understand" the situation.

So what are a couple to do about it — in fact what are any of us to do about the human bind of relationship in which we find ourselves in order to have more fulfilling lives?

There is an operational procedure which we might look to science to delineate for us: define the problem; propose all possible hypotheses for solution of the problem; follow these hypothetical solutions to their conclusions; and test them in the order of importance.

This is a very hard process to manage for oneself — and by oneself. It may take anything from a good hard look to brief psychotherapy or character analysis. However, there is need for an objective monitor or guide — a checkpoint. Whether this is to be therapist, priest, sympathetic and insightful friend (or in these days guru), depends on the circumstances of the individual, the person he is in relationship with, and what they both want and need. Certainly with the interlocking neurosis the minimal requirement is an objective referee who can re-

flect the line of reality for the two members of the partnership.

What if none of this is available — or none acceptable?
Then it will be more difficult.

4

Communication

COMMUNICATION is the means by which we share our thoughts and feelings with each other. It is the means by which we check our perceptions of reality with those of others. It can occur in many ways — by expression, movement, sounds — but usually it takes place by means of words. Communication is the message conveyed, no matter what the words say, or don't say. Our world is full of daily examples where what is said is not what is meant. When the message received is not the same as the message that was sent or was intended to be sent, absence or distortion of communication has occurred.

Distortion of communication is closely associated with neurotic interaction. It occurs in the service of neurotic control, and has its initiation point in distorted perception. Distorted perception arises out of such strong emotional necessity to have reality conform to one's desires that what one sees or hears is actually warped in order to accomplish this purpose. Sometimes the distortion is a knowing one: it can range from more-or-less innocent exaggeration for dramatic effect to out-and-out lying.

More often the distortion is unconscious: as with the

mother who sees her child as more loving or less loving depending on her own need to feel either cherished or abused; the husband who remembers his wife's inflammatory remarks but conveniently suppresses his own; and that pathological distortion at the far end of the scale, paranoid projection, whereby the individual perceives other people as possessing — and often directing against him — his own unacceptable feelings and emotions. Projection causes a scene to appear on a situation much as a movie projector sends out its picture onto the screen so that it appears as though the scene were occurring there.

Difficulties in understanding occur when a mother communicates with the child she perceives according to her own needs, rather than how the child actually is, but communication on the basis of paranoid projections is completely unintelligible. Projections are impossibly crippling barriers to communication because of the pathology for two reasons: the projector is unaware of his own feelings which are repressed beneath retrieval; what the projector perceives as coming at him from outside actually originates within himself. It is only when someone's commitment to reality becomes greater than his pathology that the possibility of clearing up projections occurs.

It is very clear that the possibility of resolving problems of personal relationship through communication has a very low probability if the individuals involved don't have the same information or, given the same information, if they perceive it differently. Of course difficulty of communication increases along with any intent to deceive, conscious or unconscious, and becomes virtually impossible in cases of pathology — without the intervention of an interpreter or some outside event or agent.

However, let us for the moment deal just with communication.

At every point in time, the place where we are physically has a high degree of relatedness to what our motivations are at that moment — in other words, what we want. It is clear that what we want is a vital piece of information that forms a basic link of communication — the reference point of who and where we are. Also, we must know what we want in order to go after it, to have it.

If each one of us could ask for what we wanted, directly and clearly, and the answer could be given in the same terms, one of three alternatives would occur: We would get what we wanted. We would not get what we wanted because it was impossible, and we would have to make the best of it, acting or adjusting to the lack. We would get what we wanted after a given or to-be-worked-out series of actions.

What a vastly simplified world it would be if the give-and-take of all relationship operated on this basis.

With neurotic behavior, what we think we want is not necessarily what we *really* want, emotionally. With the neurotic individual, it is often as though he were traveling toward Mexico at a fast clip while insisting that he wants to go to Canada.

Very few of us know what we *really* want.

This is particularly true of the interlocking neurosis, where both members of the partnership speak of lofty goals and high ideals both for themselves and for each other, while behaving in such a manner as to make sure they get just what *they* need and the hell (unconsciously) with their partner, even to the point of alienation or a potential rift in the relationship.

Secondly, what we want at the moment may differ from what we want long range. We may not perceive the distinction — may not even perceive that there is a distinction. And even if we do see the difference, we may not be able to resolve our conflicting desires. Just as I may know very clearly that I want to, in fact must, lose ten pounds, but with a hot fudge sundae on the table in front of me, I may have difficulty deciding between immediate pleasure and long-range satisfaction.

Further, even if I do know what I want, I may not be able to speak up for it. Very few human beings today have been brought up to ask directly for what they want; masochism, disguised as self-sacrifice or as "manners," is too often conditioned into the child along with his first solid food.

Since most of us have not been taught, or have not experienced, that it is perfectly permissible to ask for what we want, we are usually further conditioned that a raised voice in the service of our needs is even less legitimate. Our Anglo-Saxon culture almost universally shrinks from a loud voice, particularly when it involves an individual requesting something for himself. A loud demand is considered as a breach in etiquette, or even a sin; it is rarely seen as simply a means of making oneself heard above distracting sounds, internal or external.

The seeming paradox between self-centeredness and centering on self occurs only among individuals who refuse to see that each one must first want the best for himself or herself; otherwise nothing further is possible. The reference point in "Thou shalt love thy neighbor as thyself" lies in one's own self: I must first love myself; then I will know how to love my neighbor. Thus "loving myself" becomes the initiation point and criterion for loving my neighbor (or my husband or wife).

True creative unselfishness starts with hard-boiled, unashamed, clear perceiving self-interest. Let anyone say he wants the best for the world (or for someone else) and really doesn't care about himself, and beneath the surface of that individual you will find someone who is either self-deceived or neurotic.

If we don't know what we *really* want, we obviously can't go about getting it. So the first order of the day is to find out what we want — short term, long term, in the meantime — minimal and optimal. This requires a powerful amount of self-awareness. However, nothing further is possible without this first step. And no creative relationship can exist between two people unless each of them knows what he wants, or is willing to find out, and is also willing to find out whether it is appropriate, and how much he is willing to pay for it — in expenditure of energy, time, and sometimes pain. Payment in money is actually irrelevant; money takes care of itself when we are clear in the main areas.

We can talk in vague generalities of peace, love, contentment, and creativity, but it is only when these concepts are translated into operational terms that any true form of understanding — of ourselves or of anyone else — can occur. Actually, one of the most operational life paradigms existent in our society today happens to be, maybe not so strangely, the prayer of Alcoholics Anonymous: "God grant me the strength to change that which can be changed; the serenity to accept that which cannot be changed; and the wisdom to know the difference."

What a change could be effected in relationship if that were manifest in action by us all! It might even help us to understand one another better as well as to get along better.

It is quite true that relationship difficulties (and certainly those of marriage!) first manifest themselves in a breakdown in communication; in fact breakdown in communication is often the main source of trouble between individuals. Part of the difficulty is that there are so many different levels on which communication may — or may not — take place.

First is the actual meaning of words: even with a common language, there may be different meanings to the words themselves; different meanings in variations of the same combination of words; or variations in the grammar can make a difference.

With respect to the latter, societies build conceptual differences into the basic structure of the language itself. For instance, the Eskimo have a number of separate words for snow: there are three basic words, snow-as-ice, snow-on-the-ground, and snow-falling; and an infinite variety of combinations indicating different conditions, such as slushy snow, wind-driven snow, snow packed down, snow packed into blocks like ice, and many others with differences indistinguishable to non-Eskimos.*

In the United States we have dozens of makes and names of cars whose differences would be indistinguishable to an Iranian farmer, an Italian peasant or even to most British visitors.

---

* Benjamin Whorf, *Collected Papers on Metalinguistics* (Washington: Foreign Service Institute, Department of State, 1952). Also, Benjamin Whorf, *Language, Thought and Reality* (Cambridge: M.I.T. Press, 1956).

The Hopi Indians have no words for time or space; duration and position are indicated by means of variation of the verbs. Actually, their language is better suited to express Einstein's theory of relativity than is English. Spanish has more terms to express position in space than English, and English more words dealing with time.

There are also structural differences between English as spoken in England and in the United States. And the "hip" talk spoken in our black ghettos is a separate language in itself even though the words are English, just as the ghetto culture is a separate culture within the United States today.

Differences in word meanings and in the use of words occur between cultures, between socioeconomic groups, between families, and even between individuals within the same family. For example, a "sweater" in America is called a "wooly" in England; "bread" at one level of the economy may be translated "dough" by another, but may mean money all the time. To one person "understanding one's children" may mean a thrashing for the child when he has done something the parent doesn't like, while to another it may mean the situation which occurs after parents and children talk things out. Teen-agers' slang and neologisms are difficult and often unintelligible to their parents. Even individuals with similar backgrounds have unique ways of using language as well as unique shades of meaning of words and phrases, which is understandable when viewed from the aspect of different life experiences. It is often the subtle variations in meaning that are the most destructive to understanding because their distinctions are most likely to escape detection. This is particularly true, and dangerous, with global words like "love," "obey," "honor," where the more abstract the word the less precise the meaning. If "love" to one person means to work hard for and support but has no connotation of sharing emotion, there is great misunderstanding when the individual is married to someone to whom "love" means to share everything, particularly emotional feelings.

What a damaging effect this can have on personal relationships — especially close ones.

Confusion on the most superficial level can be seen if someone is sent to fetch a "wooly" and comes back with a dog or a blanket, when he was really sent for a "sweater." How much more likely is confusion, and pain and divisiveness, when a word has to do with an emotional quality which everyone feels he has a *right* to, such as "freedom."

All of the foregoing has to do with the verbal; we have not even touched on the nonverbal aspect of communication. Differences here occur when the words say one thing, but the tone or expression, physical movements, added noises such as sighs (or any of the many possible muscle, eye, sound, or intonation variations possible to the human body) say something very different.

Individuals interlocked neurotically become experts in intercepting the intended meaning from their partner, a meaning which may actually be at complete variance with the verbal statement. Then, if a conflict occurs, the individual caught in something illegitimate can retreat to the "exact" or "dictionary" meaning of the words he has used, going down a level of abstraction and catching his partner off-guard. This shifting of levels of abstraction without a warning, or any bridge, is a favorite means of one-upmanship in neurotic conflict and adds the fuel of frustration to any warming combat.

Actually, it is a wonder, not that communication breaks down, but that we understand each other as well as we do. It is an amazing tribute to the "radar" with which all human beings are equipped that our understanding of each other extends so far beyond that which would be possible if we were limited to the narrow communication channel of word-noises. Strangely enough, sometimes the "sicker" the individual, the better he discerns what someone else is really saying, provided it is to his advantage to know. Neurotics of a certain type catch on to each other immediately, and schizophrenic perceptions, particularly the paranoid when they don't touch the delusional system, are frightening in their lightning-like speed and accuracy — and sometimes in their devastating effects.

Often we say that communication has broken down when a much more accurate description would be that it has never taken place because of the disparate assumptions, conditionings, and even reality perceptions of the individuals involved. It is not a blowing up or collapse of bridges: it is just that there never were any bridges in the first place, even though there appeared to be. This is particularly true when two individuals are speaking from perceptual areas or universes which are different. These variations arise from a number of different sources.

Differences of perception which are obvious occur under a number of circumstances: when age is disparate as in the generation gap; upbringing has been in vastly different religions, such as Zen Buddhist versus fundamentalist Pentecostal; educational levels are so diverse that the languages spoken are foreign to each other; socioeconomic strata are so dissimilar that not only are fundamental differences of mores involved but also differences of manners or customs (from means and times of weaning children to number of legal spouses); there are national differences from one country to another; there is the chasm created by true racial differences which can arise at any level from superficial conditioning through cultural differences in word meaning and semantic function to fundamental differences in reality perception (such as the difference in the concept of time or death in the Orient and the Occident); there are differences in perception arising from sexual differences, not only male-female, but in the variations of differences across the spectrum; and last, but probably greatest of all, are the differences correlating with increasing emotional pathology.

It is relatively easy to be aware of and on guard against differences in reality perception when a husband from one country or race or ethnic group marries a wife from another; differences are to be expected and are closer to awareness on both sides. Those differences in reality perception which are recognized or known to be present can be dealt with in one way or another; however, the *unsuspected* differences can be lethal. These unsuspected differences can exist between individuals who are recognized as different or in couples who appear to perceive the world similarly, the latter being more difficult to distinguish.

For instance, on the surface a husband and a wife may appear to have similar basic concepts, both having come from the same socioeconomic level, both having gone to similar, maybe even identical schools, and both seeming to share ideas, ideals, and goals in common. If underneath they are quite different, operating from different emotional pictures of themselves and the world, there is bound to be trouble. Let's take an example.

The husband, who on the surface is a hardworking, industrious man, may underneath feel that the world owes him a living and that he will work as hard as he is capable only up to a certain point — just until there is recognition of his special capacities. At this magic point, he believes, there will be some fortuitous occurrence (inheritance, Irish sweepstakes, whatever) and he will be recognized, rewarded handsomely, and live ever afterwards as the playboy his difficult early circumstances and later "good boy" hard work bought him the right to be.

The wife, on the other hand, also on the surface a hardworking, industrious woman, may feel that life and work are synonymous, that the devil finds mischief for idle hands, and that true fulfillment comes in finding one's lifework and pursuing it to the outermost reaches. Sooner or later the surface pseudo-communication of this couple about the interrelationship between work and life goals will disappear, and there will be an inability to understand each other in important areas which will lead to inevitable consternation if not conflict of a quality which could break up the relationship.

In such a case, in fact in any case where there is a fundamental difference in the perception of reality, it is as though one member of the pair spoke French, one spoke German, and there were no common language. There is the added difficulty that the two individuals are unaware that they speak different languages. There would be no interpreter or even any feeling of the need for one since both individuals speak English. Thus the couple operate on the assumption that they are using the same language when actually their verbal interactions come from two entirely different sources, different worlds, which lend different meanings to the communications of each of the participants.

Is it any wonder that "communication breaks down" and "relationship difficulties" occur? Certainly the two individuals don't know wherein the problem resides. It is beyond their conception that there is a communication hang-up since each assumes that his own perception, meaning, and language are shared by his mate. Not knowing the nature of the problem, they are unable to move toward a solution.

This operation from two different universes is an apt description of the relationship of two neurotic individuals. As emotional disturbance moves from minor eccentricities of behavior into the rigid structures of severe neurosis, perceptual universes split off further and further from commonly perceived reality. At the far edge of the spectrum lies psychosis: those manic or schizophrenic or paranoid individuals whose perception of reality is so far skewed that they are not able to live and take care of themselves in the ordinary world. Communication with schizophrenics is a fascinating (if movingly sad) exercise in intuitive leaps and associational flights without benefit of ordinary bridges and logical framework. It has its own internal meaning — rich, varied, deeply poignant emotionally — but totally alienated since it is the one universe of its kind and cannot be understood without conforming to its aberrated sets of constructs and concepts.

As an individual moves toward pathology in his perception of reality he moves away from relationship with people. The more specialized and bizarre the perception of reality the fewer individuals who are able to have access — or who are allowed in. It is partly as a retreat from other human beings that intricate and pathological concepts of reality come into being; relationship becomes something to be avoided, and communication exists in order to prevent people from coming close rather than for understanding and sharing.

Our concern is not with the far side of the spectrum; psychotic individuals are rarely interested in relationships, marriage, and communication. We are concerned mainly with the normal range of emotional adjustment — with individuals who want deep and satisfying relationship and turn to marriage to find it — and with those cases where the same words and the same sentences have different meanings for the two individuals because of known or unknown differences within them. It is at this point that a third party can help our couple — a doctor, priest, or friend — as interpreter or translator. Very few neurotic couples are able to handle a real breakdown in communication themselves. None are able to do so when it is not known that the difficulty arises from a basic difference in perception.

However, no third party can help unless one basic desire is present: the intent to understand. That is the one necessary and sufficient component. Communication is not really possible among human beings unless the primary commitment is to listening — to hearing with the intent of understanding — rather than to broadcasting.

And no marriage can reach its potential unless both

members of the couple *want* to live more deeply and fully — both in themselves and in their relationship. Certainly in order to have fulfilling relationship we must want it and work toward understanding it, ourselves, and each other. And first among the requirements is that of communication in the service of learning and growth.

Now we have seen some of the binds in which modern man, in relationship with modern woman, finds himself. It does rather have the look of a double, triple, n-dimensional bind where, like the White Queen in *Through the Looking Glass*, the faster they run toward where they want to go, the more rapid is their progress in the opposite direction, and enormous energy has to be expended just to stay even.

We have seen some of the problems. Now let's see if there are any solutions.

5

Marriage and Its Restraints

WHEN two individuals find themselves so drawn to each other that they want to be together for a long time, it is wise for them to pause and consider the different relationship possibilities, what is possible for them, and what they themselves want. How much better to take a look at a map to see where alternative pathways lead and the various choices of scenery along the way, rather than blindly plunging into the first road that seems to be heading in the approximate direction.

When we are considering relationship possibilities, there are several dimensions to be considered: duration, depth, and singularity — or any combination of the three.

For instance, with respect to duration: a couple can be companions for the moment — being together until they find that their interests diverge; they can be together until certain goals are attained — a shorter or longer time depending on the goals; or they can choose to go all through life together. Since this last choice has been romanticized in fairly tales and built into the religious and legal systems in marriage and property laws, it behooves a couple to be very sure about it. The safest course would probably be to have successfully negotiated the prior two steps before deciding on the last.

Secondly, with respect to depth of relationship: a couple can be friends, companions, or sexual partners. Friends share only leisure hours; companions usually share living accommodations; sexual partners merge their lives — at least for some span of time.

The aspect of singularity has to do with the special nature of the relationship between the two individuals: there can be simultaneous relationships with a number of persons to whom the individual relates in a similar fashion; an individual can choose his or her partner as the one liked best among several special relationships; or the couple can choose that their relationship be singular — the only one — with respect to time spent together, living arrangements, and sexual interaction.

The conventional form of this latter preference is marriage. In fact, it is the only "proper" or socially acceptable alternative offered to couples who wish to be sexual or lifetime companions for each other.

Components of Marriage

As we have seen, marriage evolved to help ensure survival of the race: to assure procreation and to provide sufficient time of nurture for offspring to learn the wisdom of the race. Society, acting on behalf of the race, has a vested interest in seeing that men and women come together and stay together under certain formalized conditions. The addition of the institution of property ownership and inheritance makes even more precise the pattern and defines more clearly and rigidly the boundaries.

On analytical inspection, there appear to be four basic components to the institution of marriage: procreation, companionship, sex, and growth.

It may appear arbitrary to divide procreation from sex; however, they are two separate aspects of one process. This division has become more meaningful (even imperative for understanding) since the appearance of safe and widespread means of birth control. Before reliable means of contraception, it was difficult to separate intercourse and conception. This considerably restricted sexual relations, especially for women. Today, if there are no religious constraints, a couple may have as extended an interaction — between themselves or including others — as they desire without precipitating the shift in relationship which occurs when a woman becomes pregnant.

Just as conception and successful completion of pregnancy are aspects of procreation, so also is the maintenance of a stable environment for the child so that he can attain physical maturity and psychological adulthood, as well as acquiring racial background and skills. The acquisition of the skills of the race is not nearly as important in the modern world as it was for primitive man who needed to know how to hunt and fish so that the family could stay alive.

Racial education — in fact all education — begins much earlier than most people realize. From the moment that an infant is propelled into the world and draws his first breath, the whole organism is in a constant state of adjustment to stimuli — the process which forms the basis for learning. From the sounds of a voice and the way he is held a child begins to form judgments about the safety and friendliness of this world where he is. Long before he can talk his capacity and desire to grow and relate to others is being influenced by the environment around him, and particularly his relationship with his mother.

By the time a child can sit up, the amount he has learned through muscles, nerves, and senses is almost beyond conception. Even more has taken place by "osmosis" as the child absorbs the atmosphere around him and learns how to cope with it. It is staggering how much basic learning takes place at a covert and subliminal level: male-female attitudes; adult-child attitudes; attitudes toward people who are different in shape, color, and language; attitudes toward learning (for instance a TV-oriented household versus a sports-minded family versus one devoted to reading); activity versus passivity; and how human beings treat each other. The emotional climate of a household is far more important than the words spoken because it is pervasive and ever present while words change with circumstances and words are often spoken which do not reflect the reality of the situation as it is.

The television set is also an influence far beyond our conception. It is not only frightening how much early conditioning is printed on little brains by way of flickering electron tubes (what kind of a world is composed almost entirely of cartoons, commercials, westerns, and money games?); it is also terrifying to contemplate the passivity and lack of activity and participation that is conditioned into an organism which can sit without moving and be fed a constant stream of visual fantasy. We are just beginning to observe some of the effects of television, and particularly its harmful effects from its injudicious use as a mechanical baby sitter. It is interesting to note that the hippies, whose main character defect seems to be their passivity, are from the first generation of children to be raised in homes where TV has been present from the beginning.

Not only is there direct conditioning in passivity* with a completely spectator activity such as watching images on a screen but there is also suppression of learning and motivation, since material is received through no effort on the part of the viewer and no action is required which would give feedback and result in body learning. There is also a woeful lack of intellectual stimulation, and material of not only questionable but of outright destructive value continually inundates the uncritical viewer. At its best TV can be an inspiring teacher and a magical widener of horizons. Unfortunately, however, the great majority of the time its viewers are conditioned to be passive nonparticipators, uncritical and lazy thinkers, and ethical morons.

The difficulties arising from television dramatize one of the serious problems of our civilization: how to incorporate the products of inventiveness and scientific technology into the fabric of society in a creative way which will help the society itself to grow and change enough to absorb the inventions and to help them be used to enhance man's capacities rather than to dull and

---

* Damage to children watching too much television may not be only psychic. Dr. John N. Ott, a Florida nature photographer who has spent fifteen years studying the effects of light on plants and animals, has demonstrated in his experiments that various elements of the electromagnetic spectrum can change life behavior, and that the lethargic behavior of children who watch too much television might be due partly to radiation beams from the picture tube (Los Angeles *Times*, October 5, 1966).

distort them. Certainly, man as a species will not survive unless he himself grows up as fast as he has been able to change his material universe. Part of the growing up is the ability to discriminate between what is helpful and what is harmful to growth, incorporating the former and avoiding the latter.

The category of difficulty is immediately apparent when one stops to realize that it has been only the span of one lifetime since the appearance of the automobile, the airplane, the jet, the rocket, television, intercontinental missiles, and the atomic bomb; ponder on how radically each and every one has changed our lives — and how each in turn threatens or can threaten creative living. There is an apparent paradox involved: physical survival is our concern; however, if we do not survive creatively and maturely, there will be no possibility of physical survival.

However, with respect to procreation and survival today, all that is necessary is that reproduction keep in step with the death rate. Hopefully, the new "units" which replace the old will be of higher intelligence and of better biological stock — if only man turns as much thought to his own development as he does to that of his cattle. If procreation is for the survival of the species, something will have to be done to give it a little boost toward excellence. If man needs to evolve in order to avoid a self-destructive holocaust, it is possible that procreation will have to be used more consciously in the service of the species.

But let us leave the consideration of companionship, sex, and growth to a later time and examine some of the restrictions laid on the state of marriage.

Restrictions on Marriage

In addition to the overt laws (both secular and religious) which govern marriage, there are covert patterns created by the sanctions of custom and convention.

Most religions frown on marrying outside the faith, especially the Catholic, Orthodox Jewish and Fundamentalist Protestant. Church laws are obviously designed more to ensure continuity of the religion than necessarily of the species as the non-Catholic who marries a Catholic and the Gentile who marries an Orthodox Jew must both have instruction in the respective faith, while Mennonites and Jehovah's Witnesses are not permitted to marry a nonbeliever at all. The Catholic Church, in addition, requires signature by the non-Catholic of a paper that all children of the union will be brought up in the Catholic faith.

While divorced Jews may remarry, Catholics may not unless the first spouse was not "properly" baptized — one of the possible reasons for nullifying a marriage. Rather ridiculous to make eligibility for marriage dependent on which way the water trickled down a forehead or what words were said over an infant during baptism. Until recent relaxation of the prohibition, the High Episcopal Church was as strict as the Catholic against remarriage of a divorced person while the first spouse was living.

Grounds for divorce range from none (Catholic Church; although marriages can be declared void by Ecclesiastical Court) to one (adultery, the only ground for a Jehovah's Witness) to the number of grounds recognized by liberal Protestant denominations which follow secular laws, which again vary among the fifty states. One of the newer ones is California's proposal that divorce may occur when "the legitimate objects of matrimony have been destroyed and . . . there is no reasonable likelihood that the marriage can be saved."

Breaking the laws of the church or state with respect to marriage brings excommunication or legal retribution or both, while breaches in convention or custom are punished by social rejection.

One of the main restrictions with respect to marriage is that the two members of the partnership must be of opposite sexes. This restriction is not only rigorously upheld by church and state but it has been endowed with all of the force of natural law.

Why?

Why is it an untenable idea that marriage can take place between two members of the same sex — two men or two women? Even in other times and other cultures where homosexuality has been allowed — such as classic Greece with Socrates and some of his disciples and Sappho on the Island of Lesbos and in many primitive cultures — there has never been legal validation of the relationship.

It is probable that the prohibition of homosexual marriages arose from a racial taboo. This taboo probably came into being because of the lack of offspring from a homosexual union. In the early days of the race, children were vitally needed for survival, as we have repeatedly seen.

Today, unfortunately (and in the United States particularly), there are repressive and invalidly restrictive laws against male homosexuality — and less stringent ones against female homosexuality. Since the strength, almost violence, with which homosexuality is rejected* has very little to do with the production of children, it must be associated with conceptions, or actually misconceptions, of masculinity. The strength of the rejection reflects in some measure the depth of inadequacy feelings with respect to masculinity on the part of our males. But what possible reflections of virility or manhood could be involved in relations with a partner of the same sex — rather than the opposite one? "Manhood," as such, depends far more on backbone and guts than on how long or how erect the penis and where it performs its services.

Realistically, in a world beset by overpopulation and where present contraceptive methods are expensive, homosexual unions which don't produce children should be welcomed. But of course, that is not the issue; the issue lies in the inner insecurity of each man who doubts his own masculinity. Feelings of inadequacy grow with complexity of society and multiplication of problems — and are exponential when they have any taproot into sexual functioning. If each and every one of us could only see deeply inside ourselves, into the center of our feelings (where it counts), and if we could understand that it is we, ourselves, who have control over whether we feel adequate or not (we in our own actions and thoughts) so much of the hatred of the strange, the different, the unknown would disappear from our lives.

---

* The homosexual "is a member of an out-group subject to extreme penalties involving, according to Kinsey, 'cruelties (which) have not often been matched, except in religious and racial persecutions.'" (Evelyn Hooker, "Male Homosexuals and Their 'World,'" in *Sexual Inversion*, ed. Judd Marmor, New York, Basic Books, 1965.)

This seems particularly true with respect to homosexuality whose very "differentness" arouses fear in an insecure individual. Why shouldn't the homosexual relationship be just as valid and operational a "marriage" as the heterosexual one — and be recognized legally? Rather than persecution we should have protection for minorities who possibly even enrich the overall society by unusual ways of doing things, provided they are not destructive to themselves or others.

The only thing that homosexuals have in common — whether male or female — is sexual preference for their own sex (and probably hostility toward the opposite sex), and a way that is rebellious with respect to society in expressing their sexuality. In the United States much of our strength has come from our capacity to tolerate differences which may even have rebellious forms, provided the rebellion does not threaten the foundations of the society itself. Certainly homosexuality isn't politically dangerous; it isn't political at all. But it is attached to the explosive areas of sex and feelings of adequacy. It is also a stage of development which all of us must negotiate, and which some of us have negotiated less successfully than others and may be touchy about.

Freud, in his brilliant formulation of the stages of psychological growing up, described the homosexual phase as coming just before the heterosexual (the sequence: oral, anal, genital, latency, homosexual, heterosexual). Certainly, our experience verifies the fact of boys going with boys and girls with girls, of "crushes," and "best and only" friends, and complete disdain of boys and girls for each other's activities in a period prior to puberty. It is Freud's thesis that some individuals get "stuck" in the different levels of development and don't mature on beyond. However, it is quite possible that this is a biased viewpoint and that actually many individuals belong there.

What our civilization calls masculine and feminine traits (they do differ from culture to culture) are distributed on the normal curve, just as are any other aspects or endowments, and although the largest bulk (two-thirds) may apply to the sex to which it is attributed, almost one-sixth of the men examined will have more feminine traits than the average woman, and one-sixth of the women more male characteristics than the average man. Why shouldn't these traits be linked to sexual preferences in partners just as they are undoubtedly linked to physical differences of appearance and behavior?

It also appears that Freud ended his formulation of stages of psychological maturation prematurely at the heterosexual stage of development, thus stopping short of the further maturational level of what might be called the hybrid. The hybrid stage of development would be a further maturing of the heterosexual — a psychological maturing to the point where the individual possesses and is able to express creatively either or both male and female characteristics according to what is appropriate to any immediate situation.

For examples of hybrids today, one turns almost intuitively to the arts and to science. For those who knew or knew much about Robert Oppenheimer, it was immediately apparent that he utilized and expressed his feminine capacities to enhance his intuitiveness and genius. The same appears to be true of Einstein's gentleness and saintliness. Marcel Marceau, the great French mime, is another man who transcends the boundaries of gender and is male, female, or neuter as he expresses all humanity with his body. The Russian dancer Rudolph Nureyev is another example of a hybrid — both male and female at once without losing his maleness.

On the distaff side, Marie Curie, while tiny and very feminine, made masculine use of her scientific mind and was awarded two Nobel Prizes (the first with her husband for the discovery of radium). Isadora Duncan combined the grace and beauty of the female in her dancing with the aggressive thrust of the male not only in the dance but also in her "modern" ways of living. Today much of Mia Farrow's charm on the screen lies in the fact that she is as much boy as girl, and Joan Crawford revealed the beautiful Hollywood star in her movies and her hard-boiled businessman's mind on the board of directors of one of our largest soft drink companies.

The hybrid stage is probably not the last in the ladder of psychological development; there are no doubt further stages which are beyond our present capacity to see and understand. These further aspects of continued maturation and psychological development probably are associated with evolving levels of consciousness and progressive motion toward integration and unity.

It is very important, particularly for anyone interested in the process of growing up psychologically (and having creative sex and fulfilled relationship) to be aware of the hybrid stage of development. If one holds strongly to the necessity that "men must be men, and women women" and "never the twain shall meet" in one person, there are immediate false limitations placed on growth. We are all of us first of all human beings, and it may well bias our universality to place too much stress on biological differences and insist that the traits assigned on a basis of those differences be rigidly adhered to. The term hybrid refers to a psychological state, not a physiological one; it implies that masculine and feminine characteristics are both present, developed, and expressed by one person, regardless of biological sex.

Actually, the condition of hybridism cannot be approached — perhaps not even understood or conceived of operationally — until one is well on the way toward total acceptance — biologically and psychologically — of the sex of which he or she is a member. It seems that the capacity to be a full human being is approached in stages of growing, the first of which is to be totally that which one is.

All of us have seen women whose minds work as sharply, logically, and aggressively as a man's; we have all known gentle, warm, mothering men. There are women who make excellent surgeons, and artistic boys who excel in the decorative arts. Is a woman any less feminine because she thinks clearly or a man any less masculine because he has sensitivity for color and design? Society's too rigid definition of roles has often limited development to certain narrow channels and has consequently buried "unacceptable" individual potential beneath impossibility of fulfillment. What is true of potential is also true of behavior and appearance.

To a large measure the hippy-led, young people's revolution in hair and clothes is an attempt to break out of overly restrictive molds, and the indistinguishability of men and women today in much dress and many hair styles (unisex) is a healthy statement about the basic human similarity between men and women, no matter what one thinks about how it looks.

Of course, the internal condition is the important one, not necessarily the outer accouterments. The trick — the creative, mature talent — is to be masculine or feminine, whichever is appropriate to the situation, as fully and completely as possible. Hybridness makes for flexibility in life; it enhances creative action to be able to have the total spectrum of responses from which to choose and not to be restricted to any one band or frequency.

In addition, the capacity for fluidity or hybridness is evolutionarily a survival ability for mankind: the greater the number of appropriate responses in an animal's repertoire (and we are biological animals), the more likely the animal is to survive and prosper. This is particularly true of psychological responses at this particular time when biological evolution appears to have run its course and the mandate is for psychological maturation and evolution of consciousness.

However, we were talking about the possibility of homosexual "marriages." Homosexual marriages exist in fact; why shouldn't they have the same legal validation that heterosexual marriages have — particularly at a time when excessive production of offspring is more of a hazard than a blessing.

A shocking thought? The amount of shock reveals the degree of entrenchment in the status quo.

For anyone who takes the trouble to inquire, a much larger proportion of our population than might be suspected,* particularly in the large urban centers, is in-

---

* "Estimates vary, but even the most conservative ones calculate that there are 2,000,000–4,000,000 males today who are exclusively or predominantly homosexual for most of their adult lives (U.S.)" (Judd Marmor, *Sexual Inversion*, New York, Basic Books, 1965).

volved in the "gay" world whose stable core consists of durable homosexual "marriages." It is well known to the general public that there are gay bars, gay clubs, and a certain segment of society which is gay; however, few people know of the existence of a not inconsiderable society of stable homosexual relationships among the top echelon of the professions and the arts. Among this group are found couples some of whom have been "married" for long periods of time (ten to twenty years) with more creative relationships than in many a heterosexual union.

Because of restrictive laws, such homosexual marriages exist behind euphemisms such as roommate, protégé, or friend. Usually houses — unusually attractive, judging from personal experience — bank accounts and securities are owned in common; there are mutual wills drawn up by law firms which are "known" to be partnerships of fellow homosexuals (which firms also are available to bail gay people out of legal difficulties).

It is not unusual for a noted writer or lecturer to have a devoted secretary-collaborator whose long companionship is the only outward sign of the covert relationship; a high frequency of hybrid individuals is found among artists, writers and musicians, and a larger-than-average number of both homosexuals and homosexual marriages either with both individuals on the same level of success or more often with one of the couple more successful and the other a student or protégé. A homosexual union of an

---

This figure does not include the number of lesbians (fewer in number than male homosexuals but still considerable) and does not reflect the higher proportion of homosexuals in large urban centers such as San Francisco, Los Angeles, and New York where from observation and colleague discussion the percentage of homosexuals may well be over 5 percent of the population.

older scientist with a brilliant young student turned out to be extremely therapeutic for both participants: each individual was enabled to fulfill his potential more fully — the older man to move toward his own scientifically oriented business while the younger worked through difficulties which had hampered the establishment of his own career. In addition, the older is a talented musician, the younger is developing into a painter of some capacity, and this additional creativity further enriches the relationship.

It is difficult if not impossible to determine from observation which partner plays the dominant (or so-called male) role in homosexual marriages and which the more passive (or female). Sometimes outer characteristics of dominance and aggression are reversed and become passive and submissive in sexual interactions. With complicated individuals — and make no mistake, the highly intelligent, creative individuals who form the most lasting homosexual unions are complicated people — there are infinite variations of interactions, interlocks, meshings and fusions in the intricate interrelationship, just as with heterosexual marriage.

When there is too much hostility or sadomasochism involved, long term relationships usually are not formed (as with heterosexuals also) or defensive mechanisms solidify into interlocking neuroses.

The promiscuity and lack of capacity to relate deeply or for a long time to one person, which the average layman believes is characteristic of the homosexual, is merely characteristic of the immature person who happens to be a homosexual. His promiscuity and round robin of relationship is more apparent because his "cruising" is for men and not for women, and thus he is noticeable against the (majority) heterosexual backdrop. For every promiscuous, schizoid (having difficulty in close relationships) homosexual there are probably at least five to ten promiscuous schizoid heterosexuals. Further, except for the "queens" and the "nellys" and the "butches" and the "dykes" (a rather small percentage of effeminate men and masculine women), it is impossible to distinguish homosexuals in a crowd. Those whose different way of life (because of different sexual expression) is not because of immaturity or rebellion are often at the top of their chosen vocation and lead external lives indistinguishable from the rest of the community.

Homosexual marriages between such individuals are committed and rewarding personal relationships with a high degree of mutual satisfaction and are probably happier than the average marriage in the general public because they have been formed against the mores of the society and have maintained without legal bonds to keep the two individuals together.

Such a committed homosexual relationship can be a very creative means of companionship, sex, and growth for its two members. The one category of marriage which is lacking is that of procreation.

Whether this is felt as a lack depends on the person involved; some homosexuals may have been married previously (being bisexual before settling on their own sex) and have had children in the marriage. Some have very little parental desire and might well remain childless in a heterosexual marriage. Some no doubt suffer from the lack of having children of their own flesh and blood. If the desire is for children, they can be adopted, although that tends to be the exception rather than the rule.

However, it is not too uncommon to observe a lesbian couple living quietly raising either children from previous "straight" marriages or children of friends or relatives. With the mature homosexual the desire for children can be just as strong as with a mature heterosexual and can be gratified by actual children, adopted children, or "children" in the sense of students or protégés who are raised to maturity and their own independence by means of homosexual parents just as they would have been by heterosexual ones.

Of course all homosexual unions suffer from being outside society's acceptance, with the consequent feelings of rejection and the added constraint of secrecy and discretion which legal prohibitions impose. This necessity for secrecy and feeling apart from and rejected by society inhibits growth in general — except when the alienation and rebellion is used creatively for conspirational growth.

The only generalization that can be made about homosexual marriage is that it is regrettable that it is not given legal sanction. Even more to be regretted is the fact that society chooses to persecute homosexuals rather than to allow them as a minority element in the population. There is no doubt that a large measure of benefit would result if not only laws but also the prejudice against homosexuals could be magically removed. Pressure would be lifted from individuals who suffer from unfair restrictions; many marriages which flounder on the bisexuality of one of their members would be aided; and a large number of young men and young women would have their rebellious sexual actions stripped from them as an excuse for behavior which arises from hostility and immaturity rather than as a result of being homosexuals.

There are other conventional restrictions on marriage besides those of religion and the requirement that one member of the partnership be a man and the other a woman. Couples are supposed to be within a certain age range of each other and the man is supposed to be older than the woman (at a time when women are outliving men five to ten years). The couple are more or less expected to come from the same racial stock and to have roughly comparable educational and socioeconomic backgrounds (although these latter restrictions have been disappearing rapidly in recent years). Most of these expectations about the two marriage partners serve the purpose of making marriage more stable and lasting; if diversity of background is too great in relationship, it is very difficult for the relationship to survive, let alone grow.

A further restriction inherent in marriage is that procreation — childbearing and the nurture and raising of the child — not take place outside its boundaries. If it does, the child is branded as illegitimate. Illegitimate, just to be born? It may be, as the saying goes, that there are no illegitimate children, only illegitimate parents, but why even that? Why should you have to be married in order to father or mother a child respectably? As you look around, you can see a number of extremely capable, loving mothers who have no husband, nor do they desire one, particularly if their lack came about through death of a beloved mate.

There are many women who would make excellent mothers but who have no capacity or desire for a continuing intimate relationship with a man. On the other hand, many women find being tied down to the routine of child-rearing completely frustrating and even repugnant. When these latter women have children, the children suffer from their mother's limitations and actual antipathy.

Why shouldn't women (and men, too, of course) be allowed to choose whether they want to be parents — without the necessity of tying themselves legally to a lifelong relationship? Why should a woman who has had either no opportunity or no desire for sexual interaction or marriage be denied her biological birthright of producing a child?

The only criterion for either a woman or a man who wants very much to have children without marriage should be whether the individual would be able to care for the child properly, not only physically, but also emotionally. The emotional reasons for having a child without a spouse should be examined very carefully. Many types of emotional immaturity reflect themselves in difficulty or aversion to relationship with the opposite sex. But it need not be so; early life experiences, the death of a loved partner when there were no children, a strong maternal or paternal urge overwhelming that of male-female relationship might all be reasons for wanting a child and not a mate.

Many of us have known professional women who have adopted children — often from war-torn or poverty areas — and raised them creatively. Also, too numerous to mention are examples of aunts, grandmothers, friends or even older sisters raising orphaned children successfully without husbands. The successful rearing of children by a father alone, an uncle, or a guardian is rarer, but examples are to be found. Often the man alone, by taking extra precautions and special pains, manages a job superior to many families with both natural parents. The quality of care and caring for are what count.

It may seem odd first to separate marriage out of the equation of sex, and then to separate sex from procreation — as though twice removing the means from the end. However, although nature didn't intend it that way, sexual satisfaction may or may not have anything to do with conception. Nature intended that the pleasurable experience of sex lure men and women to copulate and propagate. But in our technologically oriented civilization the pressures and frustrations of modern times and the burden of prudish morality have combined to cheat many women (and some men) of their sexual birthright of pleasure.

One of the tragedies of modern relationship is the large number of married couples who derive little or no satisfaction from sexual interaction — in fact who abhor it. It is not rare for a psychotherapist to see a married couple who has never had intercourse (!), those who may have consummated the marriage only once or twice in a period of years, and very commonly those who have intercourse only once every month or two.

If orgasm in intercourse were necessary for conception there would be no further need to worry about the population explosion; the birthrate would fall dramatically. Frigid women appear to produce children just as easily as sexually satisfied ones. At the most mechanical level, many marvelous babies have been conceived through artificial insemination by the introduction of the husband's or a donor's sperm into the vagina by the doctor. (An interesting question of legitimacy arises here; the status of the so-called "test tube babies" is still not clearly defined by the courts.)

So why is it odd to think of conception, childbearing, and child-rearing as separate from sexual intercourse — and the whole process of procreation and nurture separated, if advantageous, from marriage? Isn't it just that linking marriage and sex and children has been insisted on by church and state? The very rigidity of thinking in terms of what-has-always-been-done prevents more creative solutions to the problem of the relationship between the sexes. No wonder that young people today rebel into sexual experimentation, communal living, and drug experiences to break down inner barriers. How much better it would be if society changed to meet changing needs instead of putting its young people under the burden of illegal and often dangerous rebellion in order to remedy situations which should have been rectified before they occurred in the first place.

And why should the restrictions, explicit or implicit, with respect to marriage be allowed to continue? After all, the rigidities of the institution of marriage have prevented untold thousands from having the biological and psychological fulfillment of which they were capable by dictating to them from what sex, age, race, socioeconomic and educational level they must choose their marriage partners. Also, the very state of not being married makes one vulnerable and subject to intimate prodding into one's privacy by even the most casual passerby; without marriage one isn't allowed to enjoy sex, to have children, or actually to survive in a community without raised eyebrows and the ubiquitous and impertinent inquiry as to why one isn't married — a question of such intimacy that it shouldn't be asked by one's nearest relatives!

Marriage has been synonymous with respectability, and attractive unmarrieds were suspect as to their morals or heterosexuality. Only recently has this begun to change and only *very* recently have unmarried mothers been able to raise their children without the full weight of social disapproval pulverizing them and of course damaging the child for life. So there are gradual changes; we are changing.

But not nearly fast enough.

In considering the restrictions laid on marriage it becomes pathetically clear that few, if any, of the limitations and prohibitions work to enhance and deepen the relationship of two individuals who love each other enough to spend the rest of their lives together. Despite the fact that the obvious reason for the restrictions was originally intended to do just that.

As one looks around, nowhere does one find patterns designed to help make relationship better — nowhere do we see customs and mores tailored to help take the guesswork out of what can be a very chancy choice in this modern world — that of a life partner. In searching the legal, religious, and social authorities there are very few places we find helpful hints that are creative. And nowhere — explicitly or implicitly, legally or socially — although the churches do want both partners dedicated to God — do we find anything said about the necessity for the two prospective marriage partners to have one single life purpose between them.

This appears to be an incredible oversight.

Today, when more than one out of every four marriages (one out of every 2.5 in California) ends in divorce,* the lack of attention, concern, or understanding about a common life goal in the two individuals indicates an abysmal lack of understanding of the actions and interactions of one of life's most intimate relationships, as well as shocking irresponsibility or lack of concern about the problem of divorce.

Similarity of life purpose is probably one of the most important factors in a successful marriage; it is definitely the most critical factor in determining whether the couple will find an abundance of fulfilled and joyous relationship with each other. Similarity of purpose does not mean the desire to carry placards in the same picket line or to sit in in the same administration building; nor is it common membership in a church, a club, or the enjoyment of surfing; neither is it the desire of both partners to be rich or famous or both, together or separately.

Similarity of life purpose is hard to define and perhaps harder to determine; yet it is indispensable. One cannot detect it from a casual glance at a beauty queen, a football hero, or the top intellect in the classroom. Life pur-

---

* The magnitude of the problem of divorce can be seen from the following figures: the United States has the highest divorce rate in the world, 2.2 divorces yearly per 1,000 population (up 8.9% from 1960). (Egypt is second with 2.11 and Romania next with 1.92; Mexico is the lowest with 0.50 per 1,000.) In the United States there is more than one divorce for every four marriages, with an even higher rate on the West Coast (one in 2.5 in California according to the Los Angeles *Times*, April 10, 1969).

Almost two-thirds (61.6%) of the U.S. divorces involved children, there being an average of 2.16 children per divorce, increasing each year from 2.00 in 1959. Median duration of marriages is 7.5 years, with 30% of divorces occurring within four years. (Figures from the U.S. Bureau of Vital Statistics, 1966, 1967.)

pose develops slowly and along with maturity and cannot usually be clearly delineated in the flush of youthful enthusiasms before more mature adult directions are determined. However, there are indicators; there are weathervanes sensitive to internal climate which give signals about direction.

Two obvious signals are compatibility and companionability. Even more important are the individual's attitudes toward authority and his operational knowledge of the phenomenon of commitment, knowledge which does not need to be overt or defined. We shall have a lot more to say about compatibility and companionship — and commitment and authority — later on. And we shall speak at length about what serves to deepen relationship and test out couples for the various types of relationships they might want and which would work for them — up to and including those partners who are suitable for the long haul together, the relationship which our society calls marriage.

6

Youth and Growing Up for Marriage

THERE is certainly nothing in the laws of marriage — or in its mores — which suggests that there might be some choice about how long a couple are to stay together. Traditionally, marriage is "forever" or "until death us do part"; in other words, the expectation is for a lifetime. This is in spite of the fact that the divorce mills are booming with business and if recent trends hold, between 25 percent and 35 percent of newly formed marriages are doomed to dissolution — a large percentage before four years of marriage.

Is it possible that the expectation that marriage is forever puts too much of a burden on an already overburdened relationship? Certainly no one ever gets married with the idea of getting divorced despite smart cracks such as Italian photographer Oriana Fallaci's to the effect that marriage is for divorce;* each couple feels, along with the stars in their eyes and the surges in their bodies, that this time and for them, marriage is truly to be — "They lived happily *ever after*."

---

* *Time*, November 29, 1968: "Press," p. 48.

Why the discrepancy between expectation and realization?

One reason for this is any immaturity of the participants: when they are not grown up two young people can only form an immature relationship; never having lived comfortably with themselves alone they are incapable of living comfortably with someone else.

This is one of the great and glaring deficiencies of marriage: there is no means provided by which the maturity of its participants can be verified before forming a relationship which is supposed to last a lifetime; there are no socially acceptable means provided whereby young people can have practice in relating to each other and can have time to mature so that by the time they make their choice there will be a higher probability of success in the relationship. If their families, their schools, their life experiences have failed to provide them with the skills needed to live in close relationship with another individual and with the capacity to assume responsibility, the marriage is doomed to fail — either overtly in divorce, or covertly in two unhappy people.

There certainly should be means by which to learn about marriage and to practice the capacities which will best fit its requirements. Our society suffers sorely from a lack of some sort of sanctioned or legalized preparatory relationship leading up to marriage. Certainly, if marriage is for life, it is too important a commitment to be invoked in the majority of cases in which it is invoked, and there should be prior states of lesser commitment.

Today young people have taken the matter into their own hands, at least in the sexual area, and are experimenting with different ways of sex, different types and forms of living, and the use of external aids (such as drugs and to a lesser degree alcohol) in an attempt to learn about themselves and others and to try to find a solution to problems (as well as just for kicks).

One of the problems they are attempting to understand is the man-woman relationship; they are trying to find out about sex and close relationship (or marriage). It is a very haphazard and often painful attempt to solve problems through trial and error, and has led to sky-rocketing rates of venereal disease, widespread hepatitis, malnutrition (!), and increased numbers of illegitimate births, although there is a growth in communal responsibility for the children who are produced.

It will be some time before the effects of the so-called "hippie" movement can be assessed, and the result on future generations of the communal living, the absence of sexual restrictions, and the widespread use of "mind-changing" drugs. Certainly the psychedelic influence has made an impact on our culture vastly out of proportion to the number of individuals involved.

The psychedelic subculture did not come into being just because of the discovery of drugs that take an individual on a trip — either inside himself, into the cosmos, or to heaven and hell (and hopefully back again). Mind-changing drugs have been known and used by man since man appeared on this planet; they have been used for knowledge, self-inquiry, self-transcendence, to make available unusual powers and other levels of consciousness, and for magical reasons. They are found in plants, roots, and bark throughout the world, and are used routinely by almost all primitive societies in conjunction with religious rituals or shamanism. Rather than taking sides for or against the use of drugs — or their abuse — it behooves us to take a very critical and serious look at the questions which our young people are asking and the matrix or source from which the questions are being asked — the attempt to find solutions to deep-seated and deeply rooted problems of the society in which they find themselves.

If we, as elders, had been more inquiring as to the necessity for change, more intelligent in trying to find a solution, and more flexible in trying to effect one, perhaps the rebellion which has so many concomitants of disenchantment and disease would have been able to proceed in a more evolutionary than revolutionary manner. (The same observation appears to apply also to the racial question.) The statement the hippies are making, while not providing an answer, is certainly an indictment of our materialistic, outer-directed society; it is also a bitter commentary on the astronomical price of rigidity and resistance to change; and it is underlining with a very black line our failure to solve the relationship between men and women (which probably is the first problem which must be solved before any of the others will be amenable to solution).

How different it might be, if only we were open to changing when necessary. If there were some means provided whereby boys and girls could get to know each other appropriately in all ways, the sexual included, before marriage, would there be any need for running off to live in promiscuity (and usually disease)? In many primitive societies sexual interaction is permitted freely prior to marriage. Why couldn't there be some sort of premarriage "marriage" available to our young people so that they could form a stable, accepted relationship in which to work out their own growth and maturation of sexual experience. ("Going steady" is a poor attempt to solve the problem and actually only intensifies the difficulties.) Certainly, relationships sanctioned by society for the sake of legitimate exploration of sexuality seem far preferable to the sexual experimentation which goes on — in haste, in stealth, in sordid surroundings, and always with the connotation of "dirty" or "wrong." What kind of sexual learning takes place in the back of the family car or in moments stolen from a dance or a weekend outing, particularly when the interaction is laden with guilt?

Actually, there should be some sort of legal arrangement of one to three years for a young couple to live together. It is being done anyway, from the Atlantic to the Pacific, on and off college campuses. There should be a socially acceptable relationship of long enough duration so that sexual maturation could be guaranteed and the young couple could discover whether their interests were really mutual. A number of months are required for partners to adjust sexually — longer if there has been no prior experience — so sufficient time must be provided for in the relationship.

The ideal manner to handle preparation for marriage — and we shall deal with the specific steps later — is a series of socially sanctioned and if possible legally defined relationships to allow young people to experience sexuality legitimately and to enable them to move toward maturity and the related capacity to live in close relationship with another human being first in comfort and then in fulfillment.

[95]

The timetable might look something like this:

(1) Relationship for initial sexual experience which would hopefully last until sexual maturity;

(2) Relationship until certain goals are achieved (school, preparation for careers, economic stability), plus coming to terms with authority;

(3) Relationship to determine whether the couple are suited to each other for a lifetime together;

(4) Relationship to have and raise children — a minimum of fifteen years;

(5) Lifetime relationship (today known as marriage).

The first premarriage "marriage" should be at an appropriate and desired time following puberty and would initiate sexual experience in a guilt-free setting so that the first sexual intercourse would be a beautiful experience rather than a painful trauma. This type of relationship would last until both parties were "grown up" or one could no longer grow. At points along the way the relationship should be assessed to see whether it had performed its function and should be terminated or whether it should evolve into a new phase.

The next type of premarriage "marriage" might be one which involved living together until one or both partners were through school or prepared for their careers. It might well be until the problems of sex and authority were clarified. This would involve sexual maturity, the capacity to take full responsibility for one's self financially, and the beginnings of taking financial as well as emotional responsibility for another person.

A third type of relationship would involve coming to terms with money and time with respect to a job, the full sharing of life experience with another, and the experience of progressive maturity and intimacy (in depth) with another human being. The relationship might well last until it became clear whether or not the young couple belonged together for the "forever" of marriage.

All of these relationships ideally would be for a minimum specified time so that enough stability and continuity could be established in order to work out the agreed on goals. There could always be an extension of time if the young couple were getting along well and wanted to continue.

In all of these "marriages," conception of children would of necessity be postponed. Children should not be brought into a relationship which is not assured of enough permanence to see them through their growing up years. A divorce is always a painful, shock-filled trauma. Children are bound to suffer from divorce; in fact they are usually the main casualties. (Sometimes, however, they suffer even more when they are a battle-ground between parents who hate — and yet stay together without the self-discipline *really* to make the relationship work for the sake of the children.)

Actually, marriage where the production of children is proposed should be postponed until deeper levels of relationship have been reached and similarity of purpose and interests are clear enough to the young couple (and perhaps to an experienced counselor) so that there is some guarantee that the young couple will stay together (relatively comfortably) long enough for the children to be born, raised, and sent on their way to independence. This would probably involve a minimum time span of from fifteen to twenty years.

How much better for a young couple to have reached

maturity and have worked out their differences enough to stay together to see their children through maturity rather than the present hit-and-miss (mostly miss-and-crash) method which pairs couples for a lifetime on the basis of mutual body chemistries.

It is not impossible to conceive of a situation where future couples who desired children might have to clear through some sort of expert in eugenics, as well as a "marriage-duration" counselor. Why should children be the innocent victims of the breakdown of the institution of marriage, as they so obviously are today? Also, mankind needs the best talent and intelligence and the soundest body stock available if he is not only to reproduce himself but to survive through evolutionary maturation.

With a couple who married to have children, when the children were ready to leave the home or had left, there might be another reassessment of the marriage: the couple might want to continue on together; or maybe both of them would prefer that the partnership be dissolved so that they could pursue separate interests or different goals in life. A couple should know after fifteen or twenty years whether they share mutual goals and whether they wish to continue on together for the remainder of their lives. Provision could be made throughout the years of the relationship for financial security for both members of the partnership so that monetary considerations would not bias judgment about mutuality of goals or duration of the relationship.

The final "marriage" would probably be the one for the long haul — two people with a similar purpose in life, sharing mutual interests, who wanted to spend the rest of their lives together. The necessity for providing a joyous "sunset" relationship for older couples will grow as man's numbers and longevity increase. As the years pass it will be increasingly important that society plan for senior citizens, not only in terms of centers in which to play bridge and chess or from which to start on tours — to scenery, sights, sun, or Las Vegas! — but also in terms of companionship which can really make meaningful the later years.

Does all this have a strange sound to our ears?

Probably. But only because the verbalization is new. Relationships like those described do actually exist today, and their number is growing at a tremendous rate, particularly among our young people. In the future we will see more and earlier sexual relationships — whether society likes it or not.

How much better for our young people if there is a recognized series of relationships which are encouraged — even taught.

If we find such a possibility difficult to accept, we must ask ourselves wherein the "sacredness" of marriage lies — in the relationship itself or in immunity from criticism? Who is to say that marriage — or any deep relationship between two individuals which includes sex — must be entered into forever? Who first postulated that marriages are made in heaven and must last throughout all of time? Or, more correctly, what did he, she, or it (as in institution) stand to lose if marriages were of different categories and were contracted for different specific periods of time, depending on their purpose?

And why should we buy that bill of goods — when it so obviously doesn't make logical sense and certainly doesn't conform to actual operational practices today? The question of *what who* stands to lose is pertinent here in order to measure the strength and direction of re- sistance — resistance which keeps marriage mired in the status quo and the young generation fleeing to experi- mentation and promiscuity to find the answers that we as adults refuse to provide.

Growing Up to Get Ready (Premarriage)

Before we describe what might be an ideal progression of relationship from adolescence to adulthood with mature sexuality and the added pleasures — and burdens — of raising children, it is important to go back to the transi- tion from childhood to adulthood.

Adolescence is a turbulent period when young people are desperately searching for their own identity; it is a time when all of the accepted rules are being questioned and new ways of behavior are being tested for validity and reliability. Unfortunately, we don't do very well by our young adolescents today: there is no formalized train- ing for puberty and no recognition of the passage of a young person from childhood into physiological and psy- chological maturity with all the attendant privileges and responsibilities of the adult community. There are gaps in the child's knowledge of how to be a grown member of his or her sex and how to relate to members of the opposite sex, and there is a specific lack of training for marriage.

In all primitive tribes and in many former highly de- veloped civilizations, puberty rites were one of the fore- most means by which young people became acquainted with roles and their privileges; it was one of the main definitions of behavior for young adolescents, giving them guidelines which helped make their transition into adulthood smooth. Also, a formal ritual acknowledged the transition.

We pay a great deal of attention to the healthful raising of our children, and spend much time, effort, and money on their education. But we don't do anything at all to help validate their transition into physical adulthood or to help guide their behavior so the transition is a smooth one. There is obvious need of a ceremony or a series of rituals whereby girls are initiated into the community of women and boys into the companionship of men, and both into the community at large.

Of course, the child would have to be prepared for this transition; a certain amount of learning would have to be accomplished, and certain tasks performed to show that the child was ready to become an adult. Physiological puberty would be a prerequisite, and there should be various prior rituals or teachings so that the young person could, symbolically at least, become familiar with the role he or she was expected to play as a mature member of the adult community. Psychodrama might very well be appropriate here, as well as the experiencing of some form of self-knowledge and awareness such as sensitivity training.

The prior learning would, of course, include completion of some level of educational achievement — such as graduation from elementary or junior high school. It also should include lessons from the past as to the historical roles of men and women in this and other societies, their rights, duties, responsibilities and prerogatives, how the roles developed and what function they perform.

There should also be an examination of the young person's own specific roles for the future — as wife, mother, homemaker, and member of the community (neighborhood, country, and world) for the girl and as husband, father, provider, and community member for the boy.

As much as possible should be taught about the relationship of men and women and their interaction, the roles they play, and what elements are needed to insure a successful relationship or marriage. This is doubly valuable and necessary at a time when these roles and requirements are changing so rapidly. And above all there should be complete education about sex, reproduction, and contraception.

Biological maturity means that a young person is no longer a child: he or she is capable of conceiving another life and must take responsibility for the capacity to do so. Thus, in any puberty rite, at the very beginning of sexual maturation, responsibility for appropriate control of one's own reproductive processes should be delineated with clarity; the importance of the procreational function should be explained very clearly to every adolescent; and he or she should become aware of the weighty responsibility of launching a new life into being.

Contraceptive methods should obviously be made available to the young person as part of the puberty rites. How can we expect adolescents to behave appropriately when there is no operational knowledge to offset their impulsiveness? To tell them to control themselves or to take cold showers may help in some cases, but it is disputing the wind to think words will offset passion. And what is being attempted here? Isn't it that we want the young adult to grow up as safely and creatively as possible? The initiation of a new life which would have to be aborted or which would act as a millstone around the young person's neck is not the recommended course for successful living.

Maybe if puberty rites were well planned and extremely well executed for all young adults there wouldn't be such wild adolescent flailings in the search for identity, maturity, and belongingness which today express themthemselves in every kind of acting out from widespread promiscuity to gang warfare and violence.

Not all of learning is a rigorous process, however. During the growing period, boys and girls learn through games — through playing. Play is the child's form of work, and if we are lucky when we *really* grow up into adults, our work will return to its beloved origin and again be like play for us. In the meantime, the play of children becomes the games of older children and young adults, which in turn leads to the sports, group activities, and dating which are the activities of adolescence.

Shortly before adolescence, children's energies seem to turn inward and they appear to retreat from the opposite sex and concentrate on their own. At this time they develop through the homosexual stage and gather experience in relationships with their own sex and energy for the transition into heterosexuality. Girls learn the give and take of games and the intimacy of friendship with other girls, and boys experience the same thing on a rougher, more physical basis with other boys. This is normal behavior and becomes the transition to the next step of adolescence.

Much of the best of early adolescent relationships between boys and girls is on the level of games — physical sports, dancing (whether folk, social, or rock), group activities, and parties. There is a continuation of the early childhood learning-through-play with new elements of sexuality entering in along with the first signs of the emerging man-woman relationship. All of this playing of games and doing things together in groups is a very important aspect of heterosexual learning and development.

The lessons learned in the give-and-take of games, in being both a good winner as well as a good loser and in how to play with the team, come in very handy in the "game" of marriage. The more successful a young person is in relating with members of his own sex, the more successful he will be in relating with members of the opposite sex; the more he matures the more he learns to be a good marriage partner.

In the United States, unfortunately, the practice of going steady intrudes to cut this learning process short or at least to limit it severely. There is great pressure to go steady as a means of security in the discomfort of the new situation of dating where there is little prior knowledge and no prior experience. It is relaxing to have someone to study with, to see home, and to keep company with at a time when heterosexual behavior is the thing but the boy or girl doesn't know how to relate well with members of the opposite sex. Also, going steady is an unconscious drive toward learning about the other sex in a stable environment with one person at a time.

Going steady can be a nice security blanket for a shy child, an inexperienced child, or an eccentric child. However it can also be — particularly at the earlier age levels — a most damaging impediment to proper development of interest in and knowledge of many types and kinds of individuals of the opposite sex. It is the easy way out to choose someone you feel comfortable with and to stick with that person. Unfortunately, the lesson learned is only how to get along with one other individual, which can actually be a lesson in incorrect habit patterns.

In addition, going steady forces children too young to know what is good for them or even what they want into progressively more intimacy at a time when sexual knowledge is incomplete and in a society where sexual experimentation is not tolerated. Eventually, after the couple have gone steady a long time, sexual experimentation is bound to go beyond the limits of the acceptable with the very real danger of resulting pregnancy. Most parents are reluctant to discuss the subject of sex with their children, let alone to make birth control methods available to them. It seems criminal not to teach and provide contraceptive methods to young people before damage can be done, particularly when adolescent mores, allowed if not actively supported by parents, force young people together in a fashion which makes it almost certain that a great many of them will end up in bed together — whether by courtesy of the laws of state and church or not.

Young people in their teens are too immature to bring new lives into being when they don't know their own purpose in life. Furthermore, early teen-age marriages have the highest incidence of divorce of any age. The divorce rate is at a maximum in the under-twenty-five-year-old category with 40 percent of all divorces granted to couples married less than five years. What are we doing when we force our young people into the impossible and inappropriate choice between marriage and illicit sex at the end of a too long or too intensive time of going steady?

Ideally, early adolescence should be a time of great fun, despite the trials and tribulations of being in a turbulent in-between state of change. It should be a time of learning and of expression of energy physically — games, sports, dancing, and all sorts of activities where boys and girls get to know each other better. The bulk of activities — school, church, sports, parties — should be carried on in groups with general and specific guidelines to help through the maze of new feelings and experiences. During this time boys and girls learn about each other in general — in groups, with the protection of the whole gang doing things together. At the same time the first steps in heterosexual relationship are explored with parties of couples and simple dates with several couples together.

Sexual instruction will have taken place earlier, but at this time the "rules" are worked out in actuality, and the young people are guided in appropriateness by understanding parents or teachers. Teen-agers are very curious about sex; they live in a world where they are constantly bombarded by propaganda for sex as the be-all and end-all of existence. However, they have not yet acquired the relationship knowledge and experience background necessary to put sex into its proper context; nor can they find a handbook or manual which gives a full as well as realistic picture of sexual experience, and — more important — gives the elements which are needed for an individual to achieve true sexual satisfaction and fulfillment.

All this at a time when they are just learning to relate to members of the opposite sex. How much better for the young people to have the experience of studying, playing, and physical roughhousing with a number of different individuals in varying activities before they are required to handle the choices with respect to sexual intercourse and relationship. Going steady should be postponed or severely limited during early relating experiences.

Boys and girls — any two individuals, in fact — should experience a number of different youngsters of varying backgrounds and interests so that they have a backlog of experience with which to judge whether they have mutual interests of any depth. Furthermore, in order to make a correct yes-no choice with respect to sex, the decision should occur in the context of prior knowledge and mutual companionship and interests. It is possible for companionship and a background in common to develop through going steady; however, this development may be a spurious one of habit and limitations rather than the companionship of mutuality and compatibility of personalities and interests.

Just as early adolescence is the time of gangs — when formation of boy-girl combinations occurs within the context of the group — later adolescence is the time when real pairing off begins. This pairing off should occur through mutual attraction of interests (as well as bodies) and not solely because of a prior pattern of going steady.

At this time the understanding of the concept of an orderly progression of relationships is important. A pattern of relationship should be taught which makes sense to young people because it helps with growing up and sexual maturation — a pattern whereby young people can learn through experience (from relationship, fun, and sex) without being forced into a lifelong commitment to an incompatible partner because of habit pattern, the easy way out, or the conception of an unwanted child. It is at this point — the formation of seriously attracted pairs — that the five steps in progressive relationship need to be understood.

7

Young Relationship Choices and Sex

ALONG with the ritual of puberty should come the knowledge of the alternatives of possible relationships between boys and girls. The young person should be allowed to make the choice for himself but with help and guidance available.

We have seen how the play of children becomes the games of preadolescents and moves into the activities, sports, and parties of the adolescent. During this growing up, the child learns about rules, authority, getting along with others, being a good winner and a good loser, and the limitations — imposed by the nature of things (as they are) — on himself and on others. All of this is preparation for progressively deepening relationship so that an individual is enabled to move toward being with and opening up to those he has the most in common with — and ultimately, to the formation of one deep relationship of continuing intimacy.

We have seen how preadolescent girls seem to prefer playing with girls and boys with boys, and how strong friendships occur between members of the same sex.

As a young person moves through puberty, games and activities are extended to members of the opposite sex:

one begins to have friends of both sexes but parties are mixtures of people one likes with no thought of one boy for one girl or even how many boys there are for how many girls. The activity takes precedence over the specific company other than the requirement that the group be from one's own gang.

As boys and girls get to know individual members of the opposite sex, they find they have preferences: there are the friends one likes best to be with and the companion one wants to spend most time with — the girl (or boy) he (or she) wants to see specially, to date. Thus the category of companion is extended to the opposite sex and shifts from friend (or companion) to date.

At this time it is important that dating not be narrowed down too soon to one person; boys and girls get to know individuals of the opposite sex better through the experience of relating to a number of people. Ideally the young person will date several people, with most of the dating time spent in a group setting — activities of several couples together.

It is very important that initial dating not include sexual relations. It is critically important for boys and girls to get to know each other and to learn about their differences and similarities, varying interests and diverse meshings, before they are caught in the imperative pulls of sexual activity. If dates are kept simple and are double, triple, group-type or gang-dates, and there isn't a relentless pressure toward going steady (although twosomes obviously will form), the progressive path which inevitably ends in premature intercourse can be avoided.

These are simple dating, learning, fun relationships. No commitment, conscious or unconscious, is necessary for these relationships; only the human commitment to learn and grow (of course not at the expense of anyone else).

The next stage of relationship involves focusing, which occurs when the young person finds himself or herself more drawn to one individual than to others and wants to be with that person almost exclusively. It is at this point, when there is just "one" date who counts, that alternatives must be very clearly understood and choices made with appropriate, if embryonic, commitments. The young couple has the choice among the categories of friend, companion, date, or sexual partner — or any combination of these. It is far wiser to make a conscious choice about whether sex is to be included rather than to drift into it without thinking.

The decision about sex depends on the circumstances in which the young people find themselves: mainly it depends on their age, their maturity, and on how strongly the two of them are drawn together. For instance, no matter how much magnetism is working, there is not enough maturity at the junior high school level to handle intercourse; thus progressive or extended sexual interactions before high school should be out of the question. Even in high school most young people are not mature enough to negotiate the difficult step of adding sexual interaction to dating. Even though more and more couples today may be opting for the addition of sexual intercourse to their relationships in high school, it is much wiser to wait until college age before embarking on the type of committed relationship which is necessary to take a young couple creatively through the perils of beginning sexual activity.

Initial Sexual Experience

The first true sexual experience — one which has not happened through chance or curiosity (both of which are to be avoided like cholera) — is of critical importance. It should be in the context of a loving relationship or else it should not occur. So much later difficulty would be avoided if only the initial experiences of sex occurred appropriately and lovingly.

The primary consideration is that there be real feelings of affection and passion, if not love, between the two young people. As the young couple get to know one another, they will find their physical attraction increases, which is as it should be with increasing and progressive lovemaking. However, as the lovemaking progresses, the young people must guard against two situations: a lack of mutual interests; and the development of too much conflict between them. If there are too few activities beside the physical which they enjoy together or there is conflict with too much pain to either one of them, the relationship should proceed no further. It is far better for the future development of the pair (and for their experience of relationship with the opposite sex) if they separate without having had sexual intercourse.

If they do not separate as soon as lack of compatibility is first apparent, the strength of the physical attraction may pull them on into sexual interaction. If a sexual relationship is entered into, it is likely to be abortive, or destructive, or both — with accompanying pain and difficulty. The effect of having initial sexual experiences in an uncreative relationship can have most unfortunate repercussions not only in sexual adjustment but also in the capacity to relate deeply to another human being.

After all, basic to *any* concept of marriage is the sexual relationship on which it rests; and despite companionship and mutual interests — and children — the quality of sexual adjustment between a married couple permeates the whole relationship. Initial sexual experiences are critically important in determining the direction and quality of this sexual adjustment. It is much easier to learn correctly than to have to unlearn and redo.

If one took a poll of about-to-be-married couples, asking them their reasons for marriage, after the first (perhaps automatic) answer of "love" would come the response of "sex." Today sexual fulfillment seems to be regarded almost as the first freedom for modern man — certainly one that should be written into everyone's Bill of Rights. It is certainly a right, but one which does not appear whole and full-blown like Venus arising from the sea.

Inherent in the successful experiencing of sex are the realities of time and adjustment, especially in this culture, where preadolescent sex play, adolescent experimentation, and premarital sex relations have not only been frowned on but actively prohibited and punished, until very recently.

It is wise for a mutual commitment to be evoked for the young couple who are starting into sexual interaction. First, contraceptives should always be used, and both young people must understand this clearly and agree. Next, a tentative period for the duration of the relationship should be determined, with a minimum period of six months to ensure that sexual awkwardness and inexperience are overcome and sexual fulfillment is mutual.

The young couple should talk over the tentative duration of the relationship carefully, perhaps at some point with a counselor, so that neither has false ideals or unrealistic expectations. They should determine how long they would like to remain together under ideal circumstances and make an agreement for that period with a definite commitment to stay together for at least six months, no matter how difficult for one or both of them. (Of course the time factor depends also on how often they are able to see and be with each other.)

The guarantee of continuity of relationship so that initial sexual experiences can mature toward fulfillment is very important. In the happiest of marriages with a couple wildly in love it takes three or four months for the pair to adjust to each other sexually, particularly if there has been little prior sexual activity. In the case of earlier bad experiences or promiscuity, it may take years and a professional counselor to overcome the trauma and incorrect habit patterns which have been set in under inauspicious circumstances.

It seems unnecessary to mention that the initial sexual experiences should be in the most loving and most lovely setting possible. The back seat of a car or the family couch does not qualify in either category. Adults should help the young people with this very important step, and if at least one of the parents isn't understanding, some older friend or wise counselor should be enlisted so that secrecy and stealth do not bring the inevitable accompaniment of guilt and feelings of "wrong" and "dirty."

As the young couple become more and more attracted to each other and want to spend all their time together, lovemaking will become progressively intimate. It is at this point of deepening intimacy that mutuality of interests and lack of conflict should be examined to see whether the relationship should proceed on toward sexual intercourse. If so, there should be an agreement on a tentative duration of the relationship, as has been mentioned, with a minimum of six months. Contraceptives should be obtained, and since the rupturing of the hymen can be difficult and painful for a girl with her first sexual experience (and thus difficult also for her partner) the girl should have a physical examination.*

If possible, the couple should both see the doctor — preferably one wise and knowledgeable with young people so that the boy and girl both understand the physiology of the process and, if possible, the psychological and "spiritual" elements of the physical relationship they are about to enter. A good marriage manual should be obtained if no physician of the type described is available.

Although the church and state do not recognize the category, there is no reason why there should not be a honeymoon for sexual beginners — a much more important necessity than for married partners, over half of whom (if informed guesses are to be believed) have already achieved some sort of sexual adjustment. Since the present lack of social approval or legal sanction makes the situation more difficult, it is extremely important that the relevant adults are helpful to the young couple.

Understanding adults should help the young couple

---

* It is strongly recommended that girls have physical examinations before embarking on sexuality. Often the hymen is tough and unyielding and needs stretching by the doctor to ease the difficulty of first intercourse. Also the girl should be fitted for a diaphragm and taught how to use it. Pills are not recommended at this time for young girls except perhaps the new type which can be taken within six hours after intercourse has occurred.

get away by themselves for *at least* a weekend — preferably a week — in the mountains, or the seashore or just off by themselves so that their first sexual experiences can be memorable. A beautiful setting is helpful, and privacy is a complete must. A young couple who have been dating each other for some time, who have become progressively intimate as they have deepened their relationship, and who care enough about each other to commit to a relationship together for at least six months need only privacy and the lack of guilt which adult understanding and cooperation can give them to have a deeply rewarding initial experience of sex and a firm foundation started for relationship with their eventual (hopefully) lifetime companion.

However, what a young couple expects from sex may not always occur — especially if they have not prepared themselves properly. Young people are led by way of fairy tales, folklore, and romantic novels to expect an immediate living "happily ever after" with the pealing of the wedding bells, and immediate satisfaction with their first sexual interaction. Couples start out with stars in their eyes and great expectations of instant Nirvana, only to be brought abruptly face-to-face with the difficulties of achieving truly fulfilling sexual relations.

"Is *that* all there is to it?" is a comment frequently related in a psychotherapist's office in connection with initial intercourse. Young people don't stop to consider that they wouldn't expect to be concert artists the first few occasions they sat down at the piano or tennis champions after a few times on the court. Nor — when curiosity has driven them to intercourse — do they realize they are suffering from a deficit of relationship and not of sex if initial intercourse means little or nothing.

Sexual satisfaction is just as much a matter of practice and experience as any other skill; in addition it is an artistic skill. And it isn't enough that there be love between a man and a woman, although for deep sexual satisfaction love is the indispensable ingredient. There must be sensitivity to another's needs — which knowledge and experience help to bring into being; there must be the willingness to feel and to do for another while holding off for oneself in order that satisfaction be mutual; there must be practical knowledge of one's own body and of the body of one's mate; and finally there must be the willingness to experiment, to experience, and most of all the desire to feel — all the way down and all the way up through the many levels of passion and transcendence that fulfilled sex can bring.

For sex is not just intercourse; anyone who misperceives it as such is inflicted with tunnel vision. Sex involves the whole beautiful panorama of sensuality and sexuality. Its experience should encompass not only erotic stimulation and passion, but also the whole spectrum of touch and taste and smell and sight — and most of all the flow of openness and feeling from one human being to another. It should also include the transcendence of duality so that one feels whole and full — not only within oneself but also in relation to one's partner — while male and female fuse and flow into a unity.

Even more, in the very fullest sexual expression the mystic experience of cosmic unity is evoked, and God — to use a religious term — seems to become a concomitant and intermeshing force.

However, it is the rare relationship — whether sanctified by marriage or not — which functions joyfully in that closest and most intimate of all relationships. It is the rare individual who experiences the orgasm as a transcendental feeling of ecstasy leading to a unity not only of his whole being — physical, emotional and psychic — but also of fusion with another human being and the experience of ever expanding levels of consciousness all the way to the universal.

Sadly, not only does much sex suffer from a lack of all the variegated hues of feeling and experience, but for some people it isn't even fun. It is a tragedy that now when both men — and for the first time women — are freer than ever to feel and to express their basic sexual urge, there are all sorts of impediments and limitations which prevent them from doing so.

It almost seems that, as man has wrestled nature into subjugation and thereby split away the fetters from his mind and hands, they have formed again around the pelvic area, locking the genitals into restricted feelings like a gigantic chastity belt. Perhaps in the pursuit of sensation and self-satisfaction (enemies of true sexuality) the goal of self-transcendence becomes lost. The knowledge of what is really satisfying and how to achieve it is lost as love is divorced further and further from sex. We move farther and farther from our true goal as multitudinous sexual relations are indulged in which do not involve depth of feeling.

Whatever it is, sexual interaction is very rarely what it could be. Its hindrances encompass situational difficulties, conditioned limitations, strictures resulting from social attitudes and personality makeup, and problems of neurotic interaction — even possible twisted genes and fear of the atomic bomb. However, from an operational viewpoint, the main difficulties are a lack of knowledge of what sexual expression can *really* be, and how to proceed in order to achieve this.

Except in cases of overriding love and deep meshing, any problem or difficulty (whether from individual or cultural limitations) inhibits the fullness of sexual experience. It is in the acceptance of the world as it is and of ourselves as we are — in the complete letting go of controls even for a moment — that the miracle happens.

This "miracle" is impossible if we take a puritanical viewpoint about our bodies. If we, for instance, consider the genital area "dirty" because it shares space with that of urination and defecation or if we believe that passion is "carnal" and "base" since only the mind or the spirit or the "soul" are of value, we stop the miracle from happening. People think they are free and may be free in their conscious thinking, but the unconscious is a different matter. It may still believe that a scarlet letter should be automatically awarded for any kind of sexual activity.

Negative feelings which normally are kept below the level of consciousness (suppressed) are apt to come to consciousness with feelings of sexuality (for example strong sexual feelings may bring up sadomasochism) and are apt to use sexual interaction as a means of expression. This aborts or distorts the interaction. For example, unconscious hostility toward men may prevent a woman from letting go into orgasm or unconscious hostility toward and fear of women may prevent a man from getting an erection. If anything at all other than love and sex "rides" on intercourse, the sexual experience will be limited.

As we observe the society in which we live, it becomes apparent that much of what is said about sex is different from what is done about it. The force with which sexual stimulation and gratification is pursued by its devotees and abhorred by its deplorers is an indication of the strength of emotional loading on the subject. However far we have progressed from the morals of the Puritans and the mores of the Victorians, we are still influenced by them; in fact this disapproval of sex leads back to the Garden of Eden and to the concept created there whereby the spirit was exalted and the body debased.

No matter how efficient our computer or how short our skirt, we moderns carry the split of this impossible duality deep within our unconscious. There are very few ways to heal this division of mind from body. In fact, modern man's "search" appears to be an attempt to find unity — first with himself and then with his fellowman and his environment. Those who have neither the energy nor the palate for the search plunge into escapes — either by rejecting the body or refusing the spirit.

Today we are not so naïve as to state that flesh is evil and spirit is saintly, but in our overly intellectual society it is dangerously easy to deny the body by means of deifying the intellect. Denial of the body can be accomplished by rationalization (the finding of all sorts of good reasons to justify what we feel) or by deifying the spirit, a process most often seen in fundamentalist churches or in cults like Couéism ("Every day in every way I am getting better and better") which proclaim and practice methods of "thinking" oneself into whatever one wants.

Another means of escaping the body lies in the opposite direction — by plunging into sensory experience in a manner which leaves one subject to the vagaries of shifting stimuli. The faster and the harder one pursues sensation for itself, the farther sensuality and feeling retreat and the more barren are the resulting experiences. At this point barrenness becomes a problem; the greater the emptiness the wilder must be the music and the headier the wine. No wonder the younger generation seeks to transcend the split of mind from body with drugs and with experiments in living where everyone shares everything together.

Unity is impossible for any organism trapped in the dichotomy of the opposites. Sexual experience is no exception; it provides the added difficulty that there is not just *one* split individual involved: the equation is composed of *two* separate entities with all of the psychological, biological and cultural diversity built into two systems and their interaction.

However, without solution of the sexual problem there is no real solution of man's relationship to woman. Further, unless the sexual problem is solved, there is an incompleteness of fulfillment for both partners. Since fulfillment — and joy — are birthrights of mankind, with an incomplete sexual relationship each member of the couple not only suffers from unfulfilled potential in sex but also in the man-woman relationship. Where there is unfulfilled potential in sex and in the man-woman relationship, there is obviously unfulfilled potential in the marriage.

8

Older, More Mature Relationships

Committed Ongoing Relationships

AFTER young partners have successfully negotiated the initial stages of sexual experience and have brought their sexuality to mature expression within a stable, loving relationship, they are ready for the next step.

The next step is some sort of overtly committed relationship of two people who find themselves so drawn to each other that they want to spend a good portion of their lives together. It is a decision between two maturing individuals who find that with mutual interests and goals they want to be with each other rather than anyone else. The couple probably love one another; however, it might be a matter of deep affection, companionship, and compatibility.

Since we can't use the word marriage we might call this a "committed ongoing relationship." It would last until certain specified goals — of a certain number of years' duration — were reached. There should be prior consideration of what the goals were, an agreement on the main goal or goals, and a meeting of the minds as to how long the relationship should last to make such goals possible.

The decision as to whether or not the relationship was to include children is one of the first to be made, and is not easily determined. Much soul-searching on the part of two young people is necessary to determine whether they care for each other enough and share enough common goals to live comfortably (and preferably happily) together for the fifteen to twenty years required to raise a family.

In cases of disagreement, where one member of the couple wants children and the other doesn't, conception should be postponed. In fact the commitment to the relationship should be postponed until the decision about having a family has been reached. If the young couple were new to each other they might initiate sexual interaction to experience the maturing and adjusting of their sexual expression together while they were deciding. Obviously, contraceptives should be used.

How successful the committed ongoing relationship will be, with or without children, depends on several factors: how well the young couple know themselves and each other; how accurately they had assessed the relationship; how closely they could approximate the goals set; and how willing each of them was to work on areas of difficulty or discrepancy. If they had moved from the committed sexual relationship of limited duration into desire for deeper and longer-lasting relationship which necessitates a longer commitment, they should know all these things and themselves and each other well.

If the young couple were starting afresh, how well their relationship succeeded would depend on the same factors

— on how much insight they had about themselves and each other, how mutual their goals were, and in addition how well they had done their growing-up homework. For instance, if they had played as children, had friends and companions in games and activities as preadolescents, carried friendship into dating — getting to know many different members of the opposite sex so that they had some basis of judgment about likes and dislikes other than just physical attraction — and if they had had good early sexual experiences (hopefully having negotiated initial sexuality in a relationship of love and trust), they should have been able to find each other without too much sleeping around with other people. And then sexual adjustment should be good.

However, the most predictable discovery of the long-term companion of one's most vital years is by way of a mature sexual relationship.

It is unorthodox, of course, to propose various sexual relationships between individuals outside of the institution of marriage, and particularly to urge long-term relationships like the committed ongoing one without benefit of clergy. However, relationships where there is continuity of sexual expression without marriage have existed from the Genesis of man and woman (by the way, by whom were Adam and Eve married?) and are formed every day in far greater numbers than marriages are contracted.

As we have seen — and as can be seen clearly if only we open our eyes and look — younger and younger people are finding continuing sexual relationships without marriage an accepted way of life. Unfortunately many of these liaisons are entered into lightly and ill-advisedly —

and without commitment, counseling, or consistent contraception. They are bound to flounder; but probably no more than a similar number of hasty or ill-advised marriages.

Even if society wanted to put an end to extracurricular "marriages" it would not be possible: there is too great a need for some in-between relationship of companionship and sex for people — young or old, whether going to school, preparing themselves for their careers or practicing them, or just living. This type of union, good or bad, is undoubtedly a step in the growth sequence of sexuality and heterosexuality and in growing up to be oneself, no matter how old.

More troubling than the ill-advised liaisons are the large sections of our young people who are rebelling against any sexual restriction and are experimenting with all possible variations of sexual expression — promiscuity, multiple sex, orgies and communal-living-with-sex. This experimentation expresses a deeply felt need to learn about sexuality — about all forms of sex — and the willingness to shatter any restrictions in order to do so.

It is inevitable when there is a cloudburst and the water in the reservoir is full to overflowing that the dam will burst. Blind and rigid restrictions against sexuality have prevailed far too long — and at a time when there is a flood tide of sexual stimuli and pressures. The crippling restrictions which hamper young development originated in Judeo-Christian traditions and taboos and were given the force of the individual conscience of the free man by the Puritans and the patina of social nicety and "respectable" love by the Victorians. Why should Bronze Age customs, outmoded moral standards and old-fashioned mores prevail today, particularly when the lack of full sexual experience has prevented young people from developing their own sense of identity, has kept them from knowing themselves completely, and has limited learning about relationship with the opposite sex?

In a world which splits us further and further into separateness, the mature expression of loving sexuality is the one sure method available to the individual for integration — the one uncomplicated way to join not only mind, body, and psyche in one person but to fuse two people in a transcendence of male and female into unity. Sexuality is the one vehicle reliably (if we follow the rules) available to us for the so-called mystic experience — for the leaving of self behind and for the experience of relationship to the greater environment in a cosmic experience of oneness.

Is it any wonder that young people (with all the energy of the new generation) batter at old and senseless restraints in order to find out who they are and where they are going? What right have we to disapprove and censure — and punish? How much self-knowledge and mystic unity has each of us experienced in our life today?

Young people need help. We are the adults, and it is our responsibility to help them. Obviously the violation of rules and the splintering of restrictions doesn't lead to permanent answers. Answers may arise from shards, but the odds are overwhelmingly against it. Young people who rebel against sexual restrictions and gather in communes, communities, and clusters to engage in all sorts of sexual experimentation are trying with explosive means to free themselves from barriers. Unfortunately, in practice very few barriers are breached by explosion — or without other barriers coming into being. As doors on sex and promiscuity open, relationship doors slam shut. Very little deep sexual experience and practically no transcendent fusions occur without relationship. Not very much creative happens out of rebellion for the sake of rebellion either.

However, the addition of drugs to the scene usually does lower barriers for the duration of their effects. Psychedelics lift restrictions temporarily — or with repetitions perhaps for a longer period of time. But eventually those barriers which were chemically ruptured may strengthen and become more obdurate. Unless the implications in connection with the rupturing are acted upon and used for maturing, it becomes progressively difficult to "let go" with succeeding drug experience. Eventually there is a day of reckoning. The barriers clang down with impossible tenacity, or that "bad trip" which was in abeyance during the integrative and cosmic-feeling experiences will drive the individual right up the wall with the accumulation of unsolved problems. Then it becomes *really* hard to open both to sex and to relationship so that one can experience deeply.

Most hippies become disenchanted. Some try combinations of drugs and stronger mixtures; most settle for a lesser level of reality than they have known in the high moments, becoming content with just titillation of the senses, to the detriment of relationship.

How much better to learn about "letting go" within the stable context of an ongoing relationship (even one unsanctioned by church and state). How much better to go step by step to deeper and deeper levels of intimacy and greater and greater awareness of oneself while maturing sexually. The institution of marriage was intended to perform this function, but it rarely does for youth today.

However, there is a possible solution to the dilemma. It needs only for marriage to declare itself obsolete and rise out of the ashes of its immolation not a *single* new institution of marriage but *several* new institutions. If only marriage could proliferate into three or four separate parts it could effect a revolution the like of which staggers the mind. Further, a large measure of the invalid part of the generation gap would be closed, and there would be an immediate drop in the overall level of violence as soon as men and women were able to find satisfaction, nourishment and respite rather than a continual state of warfare in their relationships with one another.

Marriage is at present considered one sacrament. Actually, it probably consists of three separate sacraments (sacrament as in "something possessing a sacred character" or "an oath or solemn bond"). These three are old friends of ours: sex, procreation, and growth (or commitment to change); old friends which appeared as three of the four previously discussed aspects of marriage. Companionship, which was the fourth aspect, appears to be a component and concomitant of the other three and more an attribute than a sacrament. We shall reserve a discussion of companionship's role to the next chapter. Here we need only to recognize that companionship is a necessary accompaniment to creative and fulfilled sex; its presence makes possible and pleasurable the long and difficult road of having children and raising them properly into adulthood; and it can turn the commitment to change which is implicit in growth from a rigorous procedure to a joyous progression.

Let us make overt the three types of unions or sacraments — or new-type marriages — which would reflect more accurately the three relationship needs. If these new-type marriages could be given a legitimate status in society — if not by churches at least by means of legal sanction — a long step forward would have been taken toward clearing up and straightening out modern man's difficulty with modern woman.

The three are:

Sex-union-marriage: The initial experiencing of sex within the context of a loving relationship of perhaps short duration.

Growth-union-marriage: 1. The committed ongoing relationship between two people until certain goals are attained, without the production of children; 2. and the committed ongoing relationship of individuals who want to spend the rest of their lives together.

Procreation-union-marriage: A committed ongoing relationship between two people who want to share their lives and have and raise children — the duration of the relationship being until the children could manage on their own, or longer at the mutual desire of both parties.

Of course it is possible — and might even be hoped — that all three types of union or sacramental relationship would be present and joined in one relationship between the same two people. However, evidence seems to indicate differently. In these times of marriage through magnetism rather than through creative planning, the choice based primarily on desire or mutual attraction satisfies only one, or at most two, of the parameters. The chances are that the initial sexual partner would not be the same person as the partner for the procreation of children or for the lifelong path.

How much more sensible a triad of marriages for confused but thoughtful and searching people in the rapidly changing world of today. How much easier to tailor a choice of situations to one's needs and to choose the appropriate relationship for one's state of readiness. How much more helpful to an individual struggling with inner problems of growth and outer problems of stress to have three alternative choices rather than the black/white dichotomy of marriage versus illegitimacy.

Also, how much easier to enter into a level of relationship for which one is prepared and motivated rather than to be catapuled into an amorphous, undifferentiated relationship which theoretically has death as its only means of dissolution without social rejection.

Sexuality and Age

In considering the types of relationships, an inordinate amount of time appears to be spent on youth and young relationships. This is not because at some point there is no further need for relationships which incorporate sex — age having crept into the equation — but for two very specific reasons. In the first place, if we have not solved a problem, we are "young" as in immature, and our solution often parallels that of youth. Secondly, in times of dislocation and flux when values and customs change radically, the burden falls mostly heavily on the young, and our first responsibility is to them.

However, once we have seen our young people through their initial relationship of sex and well on the way to reaching goals in a growth-union-marriage — having postponed the creation of a family at least for the time being — we can turn to the older segment of the population and see what changing mores in marriage might have in store for them.

It is impossible to speak of all older marriages in one breath. The title senior citizen may bring associations of white-haired chess players in the local park when actually it more likely covers a vital couple occupying their time with congenial friends in an attractive housing development for the retired. In the past, retirement came at the end of life; today it occurs at some period about two-thirds of the way along, leaving many remaining years of activity and vigor thanks to the miracles of medical science. Our main concern is a couple of around retirement age whose children have left home and are on their own. What is in store for them with respect to relationship?

The first factor which must be considered along with the rise in age level is the progressive probability of the loss of one member of the couple — more probably the husband. We shall not attempt to deal here with the shattering difficulty of the loss of a beloved life partner. Grief, with its implications and complications, is one of the realities which all of us must experience. Life insists that we learn to adjust to it and that we absorb and integrate its tragedy along with the stress of illness and the inevitability of death. In the creative integration of the experience of loss comes much maturity, just as with the acceptance of death.

It is clear that a happy and companionable marriage will continue until the death of one or both partners. The richness and compatibility of the relationship and the amount of enjoyment of the years of declining physical powers will depend on the quality of the relationship which has been established during the initial, the growing, and the maturing years. If mutual interests have been cultivated, if life styles have overlapped, and if the two lives have merged (as is so often the case with fulfilling relationship), there will be an autumnal relationship of gold and brown and clear blue with the occasional bright reds of the couple who have maintained a joyous sexual interaction.

Actually, as the years unfold, the quiet delight of activities pursued in common replaces the challenge of energy-demanding occupations such as building a career and raising a family. As breath and the necessity for sleep get shorter, active but separate pursuits diminish and the couple are left with a core of things they can enjoy together: in the garden, the library, the kitchen, the TV room — and hopefully the bedroom. These are the couples who have prepared themselves well; those who have not, either must change in order to draw closer together, or must consider separation in order to find true companionship while there is still time to enjoy it.

By the time that a couple's family is raised and gone from the home, the pattern of relationship is more or less irrevocably set: too many years of habit have gone into making the patterns to have them change easily. Thus in cases of real mismatching or a total lack of community of interests or activities, changes should be made. Where activities always were disparate and viewpoints and goals diverged, separate paths should be followed (either within the context of the relationship or the relationship should be severed) so that a bright new October can be found to carry the person through into winter.

As we have mentioned, unfortunately it is death which

most often takes the decision out of our hands and forces the willing (or unwilling) companions apart — making it necessary for one to fashion a new life. At this time the woman (usually) must decide whether she prefers to spend the rest of her life among her widow friends — vicariously enjoying energy- and activity-filled years through her children if she has a family, or through animals and hobbies if she has not — or whether she prefers to seek out another relationship.

The decision to remarry — or actually whether or not to enter into companionship with another individual — depends entirely on the preferences and desires of the person involved. If the loss or the separation has occurred at a vigorous time of life, and if he or she is uncomfortable with solitude and blossoms with company, then certainly a new relationship of the growth-union-marriage type should be sought.

If a widow feels greatly deprived of male companionship by the death of her husband, she certainly should move toward finding a man with whom she would like to spend her remaining years. There are a plethora of ways and means to manage this today: church groups, activities groups, sports and hobbies, older singles groups, and last — but probably the fastest-growing and most important of all — computer-matched dates with their relationship possibilities. A woman need not advertise her purpose, but she certainly should not feel ashamed to move with every means in her power and those of her dearest friends toward finding a man she would like. The same holds true, only more easily so, for a man.

Sometimes the individual has never managed well with the opposite sex; in such cases, perhaps a liaison of companionship (or even sex — why not?) might be entered into with someone of the same sex with mutual interests and goals. And sometimes there is great relief and the lifting of burdens with death, and the individual can pursue long-postponed activities and find happy relaxation in solitude.

Whatever the decision — to remarry, to take on a companion or friend, to live alone and pursue interests with others, or to pursue one's own solitary way — the decision should be implemented with all the force and energy necessary to make fruitful the remaining years.

Penetration Is the Problem

The problem of sexuality and age immediately arises in any consideration of intimate and long-lasting relationships of older years. Our first order of the day, in considering this subject, should be to dispel some of the myths with which (probably) Victorian society kept its widows immobilized.

Contrary to folklore, sexual feelings and sexual needs continue throughout the lives of men and women who have exercised their sexual capacities. Desire does not cease with age (although it may recede gracefully along with the hairline); it definitely does not cease with hysterectomy, prostatectomy, or menopause; and physical illness such as prior coronaries need not rule out sexual interaction. However, sexual activity for a woman who never felt strong sexual urges cannot be expected to be miraculously born after menopause, although with younger women who have been sexually active throughout their marriage, desire usually increases due to cessation of fear of pregnancy.

Actually, sexual activity should continue and be enjoyed to the fullest as long as the individual has the desire and possesses a partner who desires along with him or her. And, blasphemously but understandably enough, a shift in partners sometimes arouses long dormant sexual feelings which can be fanned into a steady and beautifully warming flame.

The only change necessary is that, with increasing age, there may have to be some variations in lovemaking — none, however, that shouldn't have been in valid and enjoyable practice from the beginning.

First we must examine the shibboleth of the superiority of orgasm in intercourse with the penis penetrating the vagina. The mystique of the superiority of "vaginal" over the "clitoral" orgasms was one promoted by male psychoanalysts. There is no such thing as a vaginal orgasm as opposed to a clitoral orgasm. This has been observed by any woman who is at all sensitive to her own inner experiences, is known by any thinking medic who knows that while there are myriads of nerve endings capable of genital sexual feelings in the clitoris there is not one nerve in the whole of the vagina, and has been demonstrated by Dr. Masters and Mrs. Johnson* in their remarkable clinical investigation showing the many intricate systems which are involved with orgasm and how the maximum *physiological* response is elicited by manual manipulation of the clitoris or penis.

Granted that penetration adds the closeness and the warmth of full body contact (and solar plexus to solar

---

* William H. Masters and V. E. Johnson, *Human Sexual Response* (Boston: Little, Brown and Company, 1966).

plexus) between man and woman (and full body contact is beautiful); true that the erect penis in the vagina feels more fully enclosed and enveloped for the man and gives warm and filled-full feelings to the woman; accurate that in cases where pelvic musculature (specifically the pubococcygeus muscle)* is sagging and the vagina is all out of shape there is diminution to the point of lack of sexual climax. Granted that all these elements contribute to the enjoyment of orgasm for both the man and the woman. However, the plain bald (happy) truth of the matter is that oral or manual stimulation† elicits greater physical response and, when combined with closeness and extensive body contact, can often initiate an orgasm of even greater depth and variety and magnificence than the orgasm brought on by the man's penetration of the woman.

Which brings us to a very important point: penetration. The necessity for the erect penis to penetrate the vagina creates a very real problem. In fact, the necessity for penetration imposes an unnecessary burden on sexuality. Why penetration? Because for the race to survive sperm had to be deposited close to the mouth of the cervix for maximum fertilization possibilities. But as we have seen, the racial rules have changed from underproduction of the species to frightening overproduction;

---

* Cf. Dr. Arnold Kegel's successful work with frigidity (minimum success with 50 percent of the cases after a course of special exercises) at the Kegel Clinic, Los Angeles County General Hospital.

† Unfortunately, many nonstandard means of sexual satisfaction are illegal in a majority of states (California for one) even between consenting adults, and even when the consenting adults are married. These laws are not usually enforced; however, they definitely should be removed from the statute books.

we no longer need to penetrate and multiply — we shouldn't even *try* to multiply, only to stay even.

The necessity to achieve — and maintain — an erection has been a cruel trick which nature saddled on human beings — not only men but also women who felt the effects of its necessity and the consequences when it was difficult or impossible. The necessity for a strong and continuing erection involves the unfailing operation of a number of systems — motor, nerve, and sensory — all of them singularly subject to shifting stimuli, changes in mood, the appearance of any sort of conflict, and vagaries in relationship. The resultant and accompanying inadequacy at nonperformance has burdened male-female relations from the very first erection. Even more, the necessity for a strong and continuing erection has riveted into man a basic insecurity which generates grave questions within him about his fundamental ability to operate as a man — in any capacity — in case he is unable to maintain a "proper" erection. Only a psychotherapist's couch could know the extent of agonizing problems imposed (many of them unnecessarily) by failure to perform up to standards (whose standards?) in the sexual area.

Man, rightfully balking at the burden and unwilling to carry it by himself, passed a good measure of the inadequacy (unfairly) onto his smaller, less muscled mate, and contrived a position of inferiority for her so that she would share this burden of imposed inadequacy. One might wonder how much of masculine supremacy (which has plagued the relationship between the sexes since Adam and Eve) arises from the necessity for erection and penetration, just as one wonders how much male swagger comes from the inferior size of women and their role in reproduction.

But no matter the origin of the burden of sexual inadequacy and the disposition of its weight. The important task is to lift the effects of the burden, which means to topple penetrated intercourse from its eminence as deified goal of the sexual hierarchy. This is not only necessary for those men for whom erection is a problem (because of age, the nervousness of initial sexual encounters, the timidity of a sexually shy man, or the lessened energy of the older or problem-plagued man) — but it is necessary for all men to be free of an imperative to conduct sexual relations in one rigidly prescribed manner.

One measure of the force of the imperative is the widespread misperception which equates male orgasm with ejaculation, ejaculation being held to be impossible without erection. This overlooks the orgasms of boys before puberty and those of older, tired or ill men whose ejaculations take place with erections sometimes so partial that they are virtually indiscernible. This equating of orgasm with ejaculation (which is not possible without erection) also overlooks the phenomenon of the psychic orgasm which is experienced by both men and women, without erection and ejaculation on the part of men and without the apparent necessity for any prior physical specifics for women. These orgasms are felt as strongly and as satisfyingly as are lesser physical orgasms. They appear to be related to some sort of capacity for reality-oriented fantasy, and whether they would qualify for the term "orgasm" within the technical definition of Masters and Johnson is impossible to discover without measurements by the same physiological means used during their research. Incidentally, psychic orgasms are very useful for therapeutic work.

Any man who feels inadequacy because of a small penis (small in relation to what? his father's? another man's? some specific vagina or vagina in the abstract?), a slow penis, a penis which doesn't maintain an erection, a penis which ejaculates prematurely, is allowing himself to be crucified by the irrational vagaries of nature and his brothers' perpetuation of myths. As an aside, it may be understandable that men might have wanted to put the necessity for vaginal intercourse on women for some purpose, but why in the world would they have wanted to cinch their own saddle sores deeply with all the myths about penetration?

It is high time that man revolted, and that woman, who often carries the main share of his burden, revolt along with him. Down with the necessity for penetration!!! Up with the experience of sexual pleasure, no matter how it is attained, just so long as it is pleasing to and satisfies those who participate in it and hurts no one.

Of course it becomes immediately apparent that some of the problem comes from the irrational feelings surrounding any form of manual or oral sex. These feelings are connected with cultural guilt about masturbation, the guilt imposed by Puritan and Victorian societies on sex in general, and perhaps with some trace of prohibition in respect to racial necessity in connection with procreation.

Don't misunderstand that oral and manual sex should displace penetrated intercourse; they should merely supplement it and relieve man from the burden of its primacy. Sexual expression of any and all forms should be explored, experimented with, and developed by anyone who desires to develop himself and his relationship to the fullest. The only constraint is that whatever is done sexually be acceptable (as a minimum) to both partners.

Or perhaps one should say *all* the partners. One cannot leave the subject of manual and oral sex without at least commenting on the growing trend toward multiple sex — orgies, ménage à trois, wife swapping, couple trading and all other varieties of unusual sexual interaction. In these times of changing modes and morals, of the reshaping of what have been traditional ways of behavior into new molds, it is always wise to try to determine the underlying force of a widespread phenomenon without applying moral judgments. The trend toward mass nudity and multiple sex is so pervasive in our society today at many levels (mostly youth and the arts, but pervading all others) that the push behind the behavior must be examined.

As nearly as can be determined, the widespread experimentation in sexuality comes from the desperate force of the identity problem — in an effort to find out who one is in an environment of acceptance and unity instead of feeling alienated and fragmented in a world of rigidity and isolation. The problems of human beings express themselves in the sexual area; they are also resolvable in that area — when the "rules" are followed and the commitment is adequate and appropriate. Obviously penetration is not universally possible with multiple sex. Nor is possessiveness, that most destructive element which can be found in any relationship between men and women. It is possible that part of the push toward multiple sex arises from the desire to free sexuality (and through freedom to know more of one's identity to oneself and relationship to others), to lift the burden of inadequacy which the necessity for penetration has imposed on us, and to make inroads on the possessiveness which forms a straitjacket on relationship and which is a malignant product of our materialistic society when it is displaced from the area of things to the area of people.

Whatever the reasons, it is very likely that we will see more and more acceptance of and propaganda for multiple sex, which means that penetration will be more and more displaced, or joined, by oral and manual means of satisfaction.

But what about our older couples? Certainly, the need for a durable erection is too great for many of the aging, the infirm or the ill to sustain. If they can only reassess their values and free themselves from conditioned ways of thinking and moral judgments enough to experiment, they may well find their sexual desire springing back to life along with the possibility of sexual fulfillment.

Older, Committed Relationships

In an examination of the types of committed relationship available for the older person, two of our unions are automatically eliminated, those for initial sexual experience and for procreation. It is not entirely beyond the realm of possibility that an inexperienced couple beyond the prime of life might want to initiate a relationship with beginning sexual experience. If both members had masturbated regularly, it is just possible that such a situation might arise. However, it is highly improbable.

The same is true of procreation. While there are cases

in the literature of men fathering children in their eighties (how old were Abraham and Sarah in the Bible — in their nineties?) and women having children close to sixty, these are exceptions.

Thus the committed relationship for older people would be the growth-union of individuals who wanted to spend the remainder of their lives together. As we have pointed out, this relationship could either include sex, or not include it. Incidentally, homosexual unions are more likely to be tolerated in our society in the older age group because desire for companionship is understood and the existence of a sexual relationship is less suspected.

With advancing age, the bonds of relationship should be looser, and probably a commitment is unnecessary. All that is needed is that the two individuals who desire a relationship know themselves and what they want and take a good look at their prospective partners with an eye to compatible personalities and mutual interests rather than to life goals and possibilities for growth. If compatibility is not certain, it is far better for an older person to find a living situation with a group of individuals of similar tastes and temperaments than to enter a questionable relationship at a time when tranquility and contentment are the main requirements.

Certainly for the older individual any living situation should be chosen with exquisite care to avoid loneliness and to assure maximum companionship. Privacy is also very important for those moments of solitude when one wishes to do just as one pleases. Living with one's children is not only *not* recommended, it is to be strongly discouraged.

However, once an older couple have found each other

and they like to be together to garden or dance or read or talk — and go to bed together whether with sex or not — then they should cling to each other through the thicket of relatives and the thin of any disapproval of friends or children. It is their life, and they should live it to the fullest they can in the manner they choose.

It might possibly be easier, just as with earlier committed relationships, if the couple weren't actually legally married. This might alleviate any possible property or inheritance reservations children might have (Mother's estate going to that "floozy"! Dad's hard-earned money going to that "gigolo"!) provided the children would allow their parents the freedom to which their years entitled them. Or legal arrangements would be possible to safeguard finances.

But whatever the mode and whatsoever the means, two older people who have found richness in their companionship should forsake all others in order to treasure and enjoy that richness in the years they have remaining.

Before going on to companionship, the hub of an elderly relationship, there is another committed ongoing relationship which must be mentioned briefly. This is a possible fourth type of marriage, which formed the second part of the growth-union-marriage; it is the lifetime relationship of two people who are traveling the same path, who seek the same goals, and who mesh on all levels. Age seems to be no deterrent; in fact where age and maturity are correlated, age is a factor in its favor. This "forever" type of relationship whose forever comes from the inner desires of the relationship rather than the outer demands of society could be an extension of the procreation-union-marriage, as with the Winston Churchills and the Eisenhowers, to mention two; it might be an entirely new and separate relationship after one's child-rearing duties were over (as reported with Buddha after his enlightenment); or it might be a relationship which from the beginning was not meant to encompass children, as with Alfred Lunt and Lynn Fontanne. The "forever" marriage could initiate with any of the other three relationships, or it could be an outgrowth of the three together. This creative committed relationship is the true "until death us do part" relationship and is a real meshing of the totalities of two human beings who are dedicated to the same growth oriented goals in life.

This is a very rare relationship and occurs, whether within or without the bonds of marriage, when two people who complement each other and make an unneurotic whole in their meshing join destinies. It is this relationship which appears to be the vehicle for the later stages of maturation and for the process of evolution of consciousness. It appears to be a vehicle whereby genetic, racial, and collective unconscious or way-past-time experiences are worked through with the resultant release of creativity which enables human beings to move toward living in their predestined state of joy.

Unions of this sort are like a beacon light and show other devoted couples the way.

9

Companionship

A N important component of all the aspects of marriage, and of the three committed-relationship
unions which we have described, is the companionship
between the two individuals. Childless couples have only
themselves to relate with through the years of their
union; those couples who have a family are alone before
the children come, if only for a period of months, and
are alone after the children grow up and leave them to
contemplate their solitude and try to communicate with
each other.

Marriage creates and endures all sorts of stresses and
strains — hard-to-integrate feelings, whether of pain or
even of pleasure — which can only be handled by the
couple together. The handling of important problems together demands a special sort of friendliness, or compatibility, if not closeness and companionship. It is the
rare problem which is solved in a hostile environment;
and it is the rare couple which survives the stresses and
strains of the modern world without some sort of compatibility, if not a real closeness.

Marriage exists for satisfaction of human needs as well
as racial ones. If the wife cannot be nurturing to her

husband or cannot respond sexually, it is clear she is not being a good wife. The same is true of the husband, as provider and lover. However, it is equally clear in those cases that wife and husband are not being good companions, as well as good sexual partners and providers, since the implication behind companionship is that one joins together with another individual in order for both to have satisfaction. We choose as companions people with whom we feel comfortable, whose interests we share, and who are either able to fulfill our needs or at least are in sympathy with them.

More rigorous demands are made of a spouse than a companion: for instance, a committed relationship for companionship might by mutual consent exclude sex while sex is mandatory in the marriage relationship. Companionship is presumed to be for those times when the individuals want to be engaged together in some mutual pursuit; it is voluntary. Marriage is for every single moment of the day and night. Never is one unmarried for even a fraction of a second (probably a mistake). With companionship there is the necessity for contentment in the company of the person accompanied, which means an ease in each other's presence, a compatibility of interests, and a mutuality of satisfaction. In successful marriage there is a very real requirement for companionship which many times is not understood in the heat of initial passion. It is not one of the initial demands, like love or sex, but without the contentment of companionship very few marriages survive successfully. Fortunately, if not initially present, it can develop out of shared experience and growth toward common goals.

Companionship entails a quiet element, one of tranquility and contentment with overtones of the cessation of the strident demands of time. We are as though un-hurried with our companion; the relationship exists out of participation and thus seems not to be subject to the rigidity of time, nor rushed along by its sequence. One can sit in silence with a companion and have the harmony of communication without a word being spoken. This occurs most often with the mature marriage of lifetime companions.

Companionship is not mutually exclusive with such active emotions as passion, but it appears to provide a different area of refreshment to the human psyche. It is best served by doing or being together, in mutual com-fort, of course, or even better in mutual enjoyment. Its gentleness is more often associated with the passage of time, sometimes even with age, like an old shoe, than it is with youth and energy, which are also associated with sexuality.

But what is any less companionable about jiving to groovy rock than sitting quietly and listening to a Bee-thoven concerto? To be companionable means to enjoy doing things together — whether loud or quiet, busy or placid, old or young, indoors or outdoors. It is the quality of enjoyment of being-with — the joy in the Now that is so essential to relationship. Without the quietly pervasive feeling of companionship a relationship either won't last or it will develop into an alternating of Everest-like peaks and Death Valley below-sea levels. Of course some couples crave the excitement of the ups and downs; they revel in the push and the pull of moving toward and moving away from each other; and they feel cheated if there isn't the constant challenge of the heights versus the depths.

However, that kind of up and down, to and fro, either-

or excitement and energy display isn't the best guarantee of satisfaction or duration in a relationship. Fireworks aren't nourishing as an everyday diet, nor is the constant excitement of possible rupture comfortable to live with. The combination of neurotic seesaw mechanisms with the added excess of energy which creates such emotional swings is to be avoided or worked through in the course of any relationship which is to last.

Companionship is composed of mutuality of interests, which means backgrounds, tastes and heritage; it is a compatibility of habit patterns and viewpoints; it is a sharing of activities and goals with good humor if not with relish; and it is a mutual assuaging of that old bone-gnawer of man — loneliness.

Ideally, a couple will have a background more or less in common, and hopefully one of similar experience out of which arise mutual interests. The necessity for mutual interests in order to be companionable is so self-evident that the point need not be labored. If there are no common interests, they must be developed or the relationship will suffer and wither. No amount of sexual transports in bed or orgies at the table can counteract the hours of separateness and the resulting loneliness which divergent interests bring. If he likes only bird watching and she is only happy when surrounded with people it won't be long until they're each doing their thing apart from each other.

Interests result from the kind of person we are, the background from which we come, and the way we have spent our time. It is more likely that a couple from similar socioeconomic backgrounds will have interests in common than one from different heritages. It is only to be expected that a husband and wife who were raised in the same religion, and feel the same about it, will find more in common than a couple from divergent churches or in which one partner practices religion faithfully and the other is an atheist. The same is true of racial backgrounds and early family conditionings. However, the most important differences and those which create the most trouble are strongly held views, prejudices, habit patterns and life styles which arise as a result of emotional pathology — neurotic difficulties which have become part of the character patterns of the individuals involved.

Mutual interests can be developed in a couple who are strongly attracted to each other in other areas. All that is necessary is willingness: first to tolerate, then to explore, and finally to be open to and participate if possible in the partner's interests. This is particularly important with racially mixed couples. Each must respect and try to understand the heritage of the other; both must see family and friends from both backgrounds impartially; and any children must be brought up to understand and appreciate the richness of a double heritage and to love and integrate impartially with both.

There must be a willingness to compromise in any successful relationship. With respect to cultivating mutual interests, there should also be the willingness to alternate experiencing each other's enjoyments: Beulah goes to watch Seth play softball one week; the next week Seth accompanies Beulah to the church bazaar. In this manner diversities can grow into convergence or at least there can be joyful (and sometimes participating) tolerance of the divergences.

There is one creative element to differences: the enrichment they yield to others when shared. It would be a very dull world if we all wanted to play the French horn, were five feet seven inches, weighed exactly one hundred and sixty-five pounds, and doted on the same book. It is a husband's duty, since he spends at least one-third of his time earning the family living, to bring home anecdotes and enlightenments about the competitive world of business; just as in turn the wife should enrich her husband's life by sharing with him creatively the business of running a home and raising children.

And when two partners are very different, each can grow in learning about the other. For instance, the intimacy of marriage can be very difficult for a shy and private individual. But in learning to share, inner feelings as well as time and possessions, the reserved person becomes more open and the partner learns the importance of privacy and that it is not necessary to share *every* thought or feeling to have companionship and a creative relationship. Thus both individuals grow beyond their own initial limitations in getting to know each other more deeply.

No difference of interest is really unimportant. Those which may seem negligible during the growing years of the family (when time and money are usually both in short supply) can become wide gulfs when money becomes plentiful, the family is gone, and leisure time has grown to frightening proportions.

When chasms divide a couple, the approach of retirement, rather than being anticipated as a time of freedom for personal pursuits, becomes a hideous situation wherein two individuals, who find they have very little in common other than time passed together and biological progeny, find themselves glued to the same spot and to each other twenty-four hours a day.

There are also situations in which mere habit patterns have produced divergent interests. For instance, if the wife can never (or won't) get a sitter in order to attend a sports event with her husband when the children are young, and the husband always has work in his shop when there is mention of a movie (and the couple allow this division of activities to permeate their relationship), how can they expect to share interests and activities in common when there are only the two of them left at the fireside? Substituting television for the fireside isn't the answer either because the couple probably won't even be able to agree on the programs.

Care must be taken to cultivate mutual interests and not to allow time or money pressures to establish habit patterns of different activities. Certainly there is no greater quiet pleasure, no greater peace and full contentment, than deeply shared mutual interests and experiences leading two people to grow together like one expanded whole. It is in this fashion that the potential for companionship in marriage is fulfilled.

But a couple must not only *want* this; they must be willing to work for it. Just as one cuts trees in the summer to store wood away to dry and cure against the future winter evening and the want of a fire, so should activities be cultivated which can be enjoyed in common, and experiences sought which will lead to companionship for the future. Thus, if there is not the good fortune of mutual interests, they are to be slowly and carefully created. Each individual must allow his partner's diverse interests to grow (in case they are important and not harmful) while at the same time exploring them for areas of possible mutuality. Rosemary might not like detective stories and John might loathe biographies, but they might take a crack at historical novels or science fiction where there are elements in common between their interests. Of course, if one individual loves to read and the other hates the sight of a book, it is more difficult. However, there are always ways of finding appropriate books, life stories of outstanding sports figures for instance, or material dealing in an easily readable manner with the spouse's hobby which will help to establish a desire to read.

Sow together; grow together; and harvest in mutual enjoyment.

Neurotic difficulties, particularly covert ones, are probably the most dangerous to companionship. We have dealt with the difficulties arising from these differences in our consideration of the interlocking neurosis. If there is too great a neurotic diversity between them, the couple either won't really come together, or if they do come together, they won't stay together long. When they do come together in neurotic interlocking patterns, it usually takes an expert to untangle them or else there can be a destructive or fatal explosion if the combination, for any reason, is broken up.

It was in the interest of assuring compatibility, in an attempt to lessen possible divergences, that until relatively recently, marriages have been arranged for young people by elders of the community. Careful planning by the tribe, the family, or a marriage broker heightened the probability of compatibility leading to companionship and resulting in a happy marriage. Even today, in remote areas, in agrarian societies, and in parts of the Orient, a husband- and wife-to-be may meet for the first time on their wedding day. Acknowledgment of the wisdom of the elders persists in many places where girls are not allowed to marry without the consent of their fathers, and the remnants of this custom can be seen in the traditional "asking for the hand" of a daughter from her father in our own society.

In such cases the success of the marriage depended on the wisdom of those who planned it and, along with a choice of mates for the young people, the elders of the community were also engaged in perpetuating the mores of the community since their choices followed the customs and traditions of the past in what man should take what woman to wife.

In the West, and particularly in Anglo-Saxon countries, couples unite through their own choice. This choice may seem random on the surface, but appears to have biochemistry and propinquity as two of its main elements. The relative success of either method no doubt depends on the accuracy and depth of wisdom of whatever chance or choice brought the young couple together. Staying together depends on the forces of attraction and also on the basic attitudes of the two partners about the importance of making marriage work, and the maturity of both individuals as to how much they can change what is necessary in themselves in order to accommodate to another person for more comfortable and enjoyable mutual living and the fulfillment of their own potential and that of the relationship.

We are not really concerned with what brought the

two young people together; we are concerned with how creatively they stay together and "play" together. In the course of a marriage, in order for it to provide a meaningful companionship for both members, both husband and wife must be able to fulfill a number of functions; they must be able to play different roles for each other, such as lover, comforter, caretaker, companion to name a few. This capacity to allow different aspects of one's self to come to the surface in order to satisfy the need of a loved one (which on the superficial level is called role playing) demands flexibility as well as capacity and is one of the signs of the mature human being.

As different needs arise in the marriage, the different skills of various roles should come into play to satisfy them. Of course flexibility of need fulfillment is predicated on the assumption that the couple *want* each other; that they want to be with each other; that they want to share interests as well as bodies; and that they want to make each other happy as well as themselves. Otherwise, for heavens sakes, why not just have an affair until that time when further neurotic needs cause the couple to separate just as the original neurotic needs caused them to come together?

With respect to the roles which two people who want to be together are called on to play, a woman's first responsibility is, of course, to be that which she is — herself — fully. Then a wife should be comforter to her husband when he is in pain or trouble; mistress in his bed; homemaker throughout the house; mother to the child, whether husband in trouble or actual child; sister when the occasion warrants; friend when the activity demands; and even daughter if need be. A woman should be able to respond with any one or combination of roles in response to the needs of her husband or the situation.

The man, in turn, should first be himself, then lover, provider, friend, father, brother, or son, depending on what is appropriate with respect to his wife and the specific situation. Sometimes the couple must even be able to switch and play the roles in each other's repertoire: at times a husband may need a firm, supportive, fatherly (or older-brotherly) hand on his shoulder, and a woman may need to feel mothered (or sistered) by her husband. In times of difficulty and stress or illness, the wife may need to turn into the breadwinner or the husband into a nurse; and certainly all couples know how shifting aggressive and passive roles in lovemaking rekindles interest and excitement.

The variety and combination of roles which an individual can appropriately "play" and not "play-act" is one measure of his or her growth and maturity.

Unfortunately, most individuals become mired in one role which is familiar to them and perseverate beyond the point of usefulness, in fact to the point of destructiveness. An example of this is the woman who must continuously and exclusively be mother and who invariably relates to everyone, husband included, as parent, repeating endlessly an initial pattern.

It is not conducive to companionship between a man and a woman when the roles played are those of warmedover mother and child, whoever plays the parent and no matter who seeks childlike indulgence. Just as it is not conducive to satisfying companionship when a husband makes his role of provider paramount and neglects to have time or energy to give his children a proper father-model and also fails to lend the strong arm of father- or brother-support to his wife.

It is a sign of rigidity and johnny-one-note when any human being has only one "thing" to do and keeps doing it over and over again. Not only does he never learn — one cannot learn the scale while playing only one note — but also he becomes a terrible bore to his family and friends.

Unfortunately for creative later-years companionship, patterns of limitations and inflexibility are unknowingly set in during the early growing years of marriage. Anything could effect this: for example, the continuance of cavalier behavior — successful during the courtship — into periods where there should be a greater assumption of responsibility; too much hard work of one or both to accumulate funds enough for a house or a child and the subsequent incapacity to shift from moneymaking to money spending until it is too late; the always stern father or the darling little girl — twenty-four hours of either production day in and day out leading the partner to flee elsewhere for a variation in the role and more companionship of equals.

Early interactions and ensuing roles which occur more or less by chance or under the stimulus of stress can determine patterns of action between husband and wife. Instances of this might be prolonged illness of one or more members of the family, cases in which either husband or wife is dominated by an authoritarian parent or, as mentioned earlier, parent-child role interaction becoming petrified into immobility.

Just as mutuality of interests or mutual tolerance of differences must be carefully cultivated by the couple who want their relationship to last, so also mutuality of satisfaction from appropriate role fulfillment must be learned so that the couple take care of each other "for better for worse, for richer for poorer, in sickness and in health."

Effort is involved for a human being to attain, and keep in creativity and growth, that which he desires with all his heart. Desire springs unasked from within; we can only work to deepen the channel and to guide the direction of the stream so that what our desire has led us to seek becomes that which we deeply want and that which gives us a lifetime of satisfaction and fulfillment for ourselves, our mates, and the relationship we share.

With companionship the desire is for a full-bodied, mellow, satisfying maturity. With wine, the bouquet and the body — and the headiness — must be set in embryonically when the wine is first pressed from the grapes. So, with companionship, must the depth and the flavor and the exhilaration be carefully managed and cultivated — and enhanced — from the first moment of relationship. To the force of attraction must be added the width of mutuality, and the depth of experience, and the growing together of age and mellowness. All these are aided by mutual participation in the universals of nature — ocean, mountain, tree, and sky — and the transporting harmonies of music, or the universals of any soaring beyond the limitations of one to the infinity of unity. The elements are gathered and cultivated and joined together. Then the mixture must be allowed to age and mellow with the years, coming into the fullness of its body and the complete spectrum of its delight-giving capacities along with its growth into maturity.

10

Growth, Commitment, Authority and Pain

Growth, or Change Toward Maturity

THE fourth aspect of marriage is growth. The necessity for growth and development is an integral part of the human condition and a requirement for any creative relationship. Growth is used here in the sense of develop, evolve, and mature, not in the attainment of full size or biological maturity. How well we solve the problems (by growing) that life prescribes for us determines how amply we fulfill our potential and how profoundly we participate in the experience.

Because time is usually associated with growth, age or biological maturity is often equated with psychological maturity; but there may be little or no correspondence. Many marriages, for instance, are unions of grown bodies but of infant psyches; and all of us have observed age being associated with foolishness rather than wisdom. However, if one integrates the experiences which come with passing years, the correlation between age and maturity should be high. The educational process, the responsibilities of holding a job, successful (and unsuccessful!) interaction with other individuals, all tend to grow one up.

In order to relate deeply and successfully with another human being, as in marriage, an individual must have developed to the point where he is able both to want and to work to achieve something for someone other than himself. This presupposes the relinquishment of a certain amount of the omnipotence and narcissism of childhood. The limitation of one's self for another individual or in the service of long-range goals is a mature faculty, and is related to the capacity to accept responsibility and to sustain frustration. No marriage can really succeed without its partners having the capacity to accept responsibility and to discipline themselves. On the other hand, no marriage can be really rewarding without the capacity to open up to and share with one's mate. The capacity for love, opening, sharing, and letting go of barriers, is a maturity which unfortunately many people never attain.

The growth part of marriage, or a committed relationship, presupposes a certain amount of maturity to begin with: the maturity necessary to take responsibility for problems and to make changes in oneself when limitations become apparent. This has several operational levels: first, environmental adjustment changes, such as always screwing the top on the toothpaste because someone else is also using it; second, the shifts necessary to meet changing conditions of life brought about by living with another person, adjustments of habits and compromises of taste; third and finally, the growth which is an integral part of true marriage, the deep change which individuals who are headed toward fulfillment of their own potential must make to eliminate their lacks and transform their limitations without harm to their partner.

There are three areas of growth, and all must be compatible: his growth, her growth, and growth of the relationship. All three growths can be compatible only when they are all in the direction of creative fulfillment of potential.

The committed relationship of marriage (sanctified or not) is a particularly apt vehicle, a particularly forceful means, for aiding the task of evolving maturity. However, the couple must want to change and grow. The desire to grow or at least the willingness to change is the essential feature of a relationship which will mature.

Creative growth is impossible when individuals are married to their interlocking neuroses and fused dependencies more than they are to each other. By definition, interlocking neurosis means commitment to the status quo: an agreement that each of the partners will fill the other's lacks, and both of them will fight off any intruder into the arrangement. A peculiarly difficult double bind arises, both with individuals and with marriage, when life insists on growth and change and the couple are dedicated to its avoidance.

The presence of growth in individuals and in a marriage is the signal of a certain amount of maturity and a certain depth of relationship; it is also the sign of one of the most important and most neglected psychological mechanisms: commitment. The true understanding of valid commitment along with the understanding of creative revolution (change in the service of evolution) might very well bring into being that giant leap in awareness which is so necessary for man today in order that he reverse his headlong rush toward the precipice of racial annihilation.

How does the process work in marriage? In order to have a relationship where each of the couple will have maximum opportunity for growth toward his or her own potential, the ideal is two people who love each other, who more or less accept responsibility for themselves and at the least are willing to change when the necessity is shown them, who want the best for each other, and who will work toward the good of the relationship. These are either overt or covert commitments.

The first months of the courtship, the excitement of the marriage, and the progressive intimacy between two people who love each other suppresses differences between them and obscures the conflicts which arise because of such differences. This early "peak" period is a fore-taste, a preview, of how things can be all the time between a devoted couple after they have worked through their basic divergences and life problems.

At some point after the honeymoon, however, the differences will begin to manifest themselves: individual differences of preference, background, and heritage. Many of these will be minor and can be adjusted without the couple falling out of step. However, a good number will signal real divergences and will create trouble if they are not dealt with as soon as possible.

At this point, if the couple is committed to each other and to the relationship, they will move toward solving the problem. Each partner will take responsibility for his or her contribution to the difficulties; each will take responsibility for his own necessity to change — in the service of developing both themselves and the marriage;

and each will take the appropriate action toward his own change. The ideal sequence results in growth on the part of both along with growth of the relationship.

This is a large order, particularly when the change required lies in the area of habit patterns and personality traits which are deeply embedded or to which the individual is attached. Change is a very painful process and our psyches often put blinders on us so that we are unable to see what we must do to change. If the course of action is not clear, the couple should seek the help of a third person, friend or professional, to clarify the situation so that there is agreement with respect to the specific actions required.

When the change required bears on the area of basic dependencies and inadequacies, it is virtually impossible for the couple to effect the actions by themselves; it takes real help and guidance to steer two people through fundamental changes of character. It is impossible to manage the needed changes, no matter how skillful the help, if there is not a greater commitment on the part of the couple to the relationship and to each other than to themselves (than to the immature and neurotic parts of themselves, that is). In other words, the necessary commitment must be to growth.

In the development of a relationship which is to endure, whether it be marriage or a committed ongoing relationship, there are certain periods of difficulty which must be understood as part of the process of maturation and not as a rupture of relationship. These cannot be negotiated without a mutual commitment to growth.

The first period has been mentioned — following the honeymoon — when two individuals with all of their unique differences are settling down to live with each other. The halo of courtship and the honeymoon rainbow have faded in the strong light of everyday living as problems and stresses of life interact with personality differences which had been obscured by the rosy glow of romance. Actually, it takes a certain amount of adjustment just to the operational details of living with a new roommate; how much more difficult are the adjustments to the initial phase of a lifelong relationship! Minor decisions about hours, lights, noise, and activities with a roommate of six months become much more critical when they involve lifelong changes.

If our couple have made their preparations well, if they are in love (or deeply desirous of relationship), if they are relatively mature, and if they have mutual interests and backgrounds or are willing to work toward them, they will negotiate the change and growth required. This first adjustment is the change from two separate individuals with two ways of life to two individuals in relationship, and the relationship is more important than separateness. He shifts from the romantic suitor to the responsible breadwinner (without being any less loving); she shifts from the fashion-plate date to the competent homemaker (without detriment to her appearance); both adjust their tastes and interests in a series of compromises so that their activities are mutually rewarding.

The next time of difficulty is when the couple shift from separate but related individuals to a unity of identity, a shift where their separate identities, which have been meshed in the growing relationship, are superseded in a subtle way by the relationship identity of which they are each part. This shift or the beginnings of the difficulties associated with it occurs somewhere around the second to third year of marriage (a time when one-third of all marriages go on the rocks and most affairs, which usually survive at most three years, are in difficulty). It apparently involves the appearance and working through (if the relationship is to be successful) of basic dependencies in each member of the couple. This is a difficult time and is signaled by more conflicts than usual and an *apparent* (only apparent) lessening and cooling of sexual desires. A great many young people mistakenly assume that they have fallen out of love and either start looking for another partner or settle for sexual activity which is greatly diminished from their accustomed pattern.

This period is critical; it is imperative that the young people realize that the diminishment of gratifying sex is only temporary and signals unsolved dependency problems which are surfacing in order to be dealt with. It is far easier if the young couple have some professional help in the form of marital counseling at this time so the dislocations and difficulties of their relationship are not too lengthy or severe.

This is a time when the couple are in the throes of working out earlier incorrect family patterns of interaction, and often it seems almost hopeless. Where before there may have been relatively few areas of disagreement, now they seem at odds on almost everything. Both feel inadequate and feel the push to find something or someone to bolster their ego. Sexual relations seem to deteriorate further. This is the period of working through whatever interlocking neurosis is present in their relationship.

Some of the problems dealt with at this time are deeper

levels of hostility, male supremacy and its response in female passivity or female supremacy, possessiveness, passivity and dependency. These latter problems may have their roots in narcissism and feelings of omnipotence, both of which are really worked out only as they are "lived through." In other words as an individual becomes more mature and finds his own valid path in life, narcissism falls away and the omnipotence shrinks to reality size, and both can be dealt with.

If the couple will be patient and stay oriented toward the overall relationship and the necessity for growth and if they will obtain professional help if necessary to negotiate this period without too long a time of too much pain, they will find that, as the problems begin resolving, their sexuality returns. They begin to see each other with entirely fresh, new eyes. As the problems are worked on and solutions are effected, their relationship has all the excitement of a second honeymoon, and they find their marriage at an entirely new level.

This shift to oneness of relationship from two individuals in relationship is postponed if children come shortly after the couple are married. It is the appearance of children which occasions another stress period of critical change in the marriage. Children are more easily incorporated into a marriage where unity of relationship has been reached than into one of a two-individuals-in-relationship. A third force can bring disequilibrium when two original forces have not reached resolution or stability; it is more difficult to throw a stable unified base out of kilter with an additional element.

In a way, the growth necessary to manage the relationship changes to incorporate children is of the same cate-

gory as the shift where the relationship becomes primary over the two individuals because of the necessity
to deal with dependency needs of the couple. There is
not only the obvious shift in the family budget and in
living space and time which the birth of a baby precipi-
tates, but a helpless creature suddenly appears who must
be totally cared for. Any unsolved dependency of either
mother or father is activated, and the appearance of a
third member in a two-member structure necessitates a
whole new balance between the original two, thus awak-
ening possessiveness, competition, and any unresolved
oedipal difficulties.

The appearance of a child puts severe although often
unrecognized stress on a relationship, no matter at what
point the child appears. The greater the immaturity of
the couple, the greater the stress. A postpartum depres-
sion is not uncommon for a new mother; "blue days" in
the hospital are routine. Also it is not unheard of for a
prospective father to go into a tailspin and even to make
a suicide attempt (usually covert) because of feelings of
hopelessness at the threat to his interlocking neurosis
with his wife and their interdependency needs which the
baby's appearance threatens.

Just as irrational "cravings" and actions occur and are
tolerated in a pregnant woman, so also uncommon and
unusual actions on the part of the prospective father
occur — although they are not so easily tolerated by
wives and society. There is often an increase in drinking
and nights out, unaccustomed and irregular behavior on
the job, and even running around with other women
(affairs with other women are very common during times
of pregnancy of a wife, particularly if she is not aware of
and careful to satisfy her husband sexually).

Needless to say, when the child is unplanned for — and unwanted — the difficulties are magnified.

There are two additional areas of necessity-provoked change and growth in marriage: what can be called a life purpose crisis, when the couple come to the same goals and general way of life; and a long haul crisis, when physical energies are fading, the point of no return has been passed, and the couple must face each other and what they have or have not made of their lives. In the first case, there is time for the drastic change which makes possible either life together or separation so that the couple may each seek another partner for the long haul. This crisis involves a change: there must be creation of a growth-union type relationship or separation of the couple (divorce?) and the formation of a new relationship. It is a period of reevaluation and assessment in order to have a true merging of life goals and life path, or else there must be a shift to another partner.

With respect to the "long haul" crisis, there may be neither time nor energy for drastic change, either in their lives together or in a separation for life with someone else. If there is not sufficient time, there can only be movement toward more companionable living and a shift toward mutuality and comfort without the growth element.

None of these critical growth-necessity periods can be negotiated unless both members of the marriage want the relationship more than their own way. None are easily negotiable; and most require help from outside, even if only through the aid of an objective friend who can act as a reality check for the two individuals. It seems redundant to repeat that in case of serious problems,

[167]

professional help will be required. However, even professional help will be unavailing if there is not a commitment on both sides to the relationship — first and foremost.

Actually, commitment is the central concept on which any marriage turns. It is a concept which is not often evoked and is very little understood in the everyday life of the twentieth century. In fact, the idea of mutual dedication and commitment of a man and a woman to each other "in the eyes of God and this company" has become isolated and fossilized in the rituals of the church and has ceased to be understood as deeply meaningful motivation in relationship. Our society appears to have grown away from the knowledge and awareness of its implications, to the detriment of all of us. Increasingly we see the phenomenon of the pursuit of "relationship" with all of the fervor usually associated with those dedicated to God, but its practice with all the fickleness of the Devil because of the lack of understanding of the role that commitment can play with respect to setting direction and aiding in perseverance and the overcoming of obstacles.

It is perhaps understandable why individuals have overlooked the value of what might be called a double-committed marriage — commitment of the two individuals to each other and to the same goal — which is an enormous aid in the process of change toward maturity. However, it is hard to understand why institutions interested in evolution and maturity (particularly the churches) have not recognized the importance of this type of committed relationship as a vehicle for fulfilling life and deep human rewards for the participants. Further, a committed marriage relationship can be used as a vehicle for the religious path — for the experiencing of God.* Perhaps the myopia of the churches comes from their inflexible perception of marriage as a vehicle for procreation rather than as a relationship for the mutual growth and evolution of its members and the fulfillment of their potential.

Commitment and Authority

To commit — to give oneself wholly to something. Commitment — an integrated action which is sadly lacking with individual modern man but found in devastating force with collective man in the service of submission of the individual integrity and independence to an ideal (Communism) or to the larger whole of the state (nationalism leading to the disastrous finale of National Socialism or Nazism).

Commitment is not easily come by: it presupposes an individual who has a sense of his own identity and integrity and an intuitive feeling for the necessity for singleness of direction, plus an intuitive feeling about what the creative direction is. Perhaps commitment is best arrived at today through the negative means of learning what has not been satisfying, what has not worked, what has led toward dissolution rather than integration, and what has been the path of pain.

Whatever the means for its beginning, it appears to be the necessary, if not the sufficient, precursor for the find-

---

* In this Atomic Age of Anxiety, it is far likelier that "sainthood" will be attained by two deeply committed individuals traveling all the way together along the path of removal of barriers to creativity than by any other means.

ing of meaning (and direction) in the chaotic world of today. Paradoxically, even if an understanding of the necessity for commitment arises in the intellect and is accompanied by desire, commitment is not under control of the will. (Will is here considered an attribute of the conscious mind.) There may be a conscious, cerebral wish, but the wish may have no relationship or congruence to the deep instinctive push which most surely and deeply motivates us. We have as many levels as an onion has layers, and they may be mostly of one piece, or each one can be at variance with every other one. The trick is to get them all into unison!

"Purity of heart is to will one thing" is the implication in Kierkegaard.* And certainly, movement of the organism toward its fulfillment must be part of the "one thing." Indeed, if all of our levels were in harmony they would be focused toward our growth toward fulfillment of our potential — and our commitment would be to go as far as possible toward reaching the goal. To say it differently: lack of conflict is in wanting only one direction and that with all the levels of one's being. The only possible direction — when all are combined in one — is toward unity.

The first prod along the path toward integration and fulfillment usually comes from pain: the individual finds himself hurting psychically. In order to remove the pain he pauses and tries to see what is causing it. Obvious difficulties he changes immediately; he is able to find and remove these first-level emotional pains if his warning

---

* Sören Kierkegaard, *Purity of Heart* (New York: Harper and Brothers, 1938).

signal is in good working order. However, if the pain persists, and if he exhausts all other possibilities, he will eventually see that it is a lack of movement toward growth and maturity which is causing the difficulty.

The first step toward growth or change is this recognition. From the recognition comes the intellectual commitment (decision) to move in the direction which is intended for him to go. Intellectual commitment deepens into emotional commitment as the action of movement takes place. At a certain point the commitment becomes total, a process achieved not easily nor without pain but wherein, paradoxically, lies the only freedom. And then it is as if the process takes care of itself and "lives" the individual rather than vice versa.

This is a long and arduous process, the deepening of the intellectual decision to move toward fulfillment of one's potential into an emotional commitment which operates on its own. When the emotional commitment comes into being we then "want" to move toward our potential as well as thinking that is the best thing to do. Desire has entered to strengthen the pale resolve of the intellect; we have the force of the pleasure principle operating to help us.

Marriage, or the committed ongoing relationship, is the vehicle which helps us move toward our own fulfillment by means of growth and change. In turn, commitment makes it possible for the choice to be toward growth when there are difficulties in relationship or when change is required on the part of one or both individuals. It is the greater commitment to the relationship which helps the individual endure the pain of change; it is in the commitment of the relationship to growth and the fulfillment of both individuals' potential which enables the relationship itself to change and mature and to provide an ever more creative matrix for the two evolving participants.

This process of double commitment, of both of the individuals to the relationship, and of the relationship to growth, is one of the fastest and most creative mechanisms for change that mankind today has available to meet the demands for immediate and fundamental change. A double-committed marriage is one whereby the individuals are committed to each other and to the same goal. The goal to which the two individuals are committed must be the removal of any and all barriers toward their own and their mate's fulfillment of potential. Otherwise the double commitment will not work toward allowing both individual's growth toward fulfillment of their potential (without impingement on each other) while the relationship itself at the same time deepens and matures. All of the disparate goals of man, woman, and relationship come into unity only at that point where all movement is toward fulfillment of potential, not the least of which potential is abundance and joy.

In all of our discussion of marriage and commitment, we have not once raised the question of authority.

Authority — fighting words today when so often one survives only by means of rebellion, rebellion against neurotic parents, rebellion against limiting environment and invalid burdens, rebellion against a world racing toward self-destruction.

The question of authority at first seems to have very little to do with a consideration of marriage — unless the question arises as to how to handle children. But authority is actually vitally connected to marriage through commitment. The separation of the concept of commitment from that of authority is a false division: the concept of commitment includes as one of its intrinsic aspects an individual's appropriate relationship to authority.

Relationship to authority? Authority to what? The only valid authority is that of reality: the authority of the world as it is, of things as they are. Let us avoid any intellectual discussion of relative realities, ultimate reality versus operational reality, your reality versus my reality, or any other semantic games which serve to entertain philosophers as kriegspiel is entertaining play for mathematicians.

The authority of reality is that authority which arises out of the context of a situation; it arises from the goal which is set and the rules of motion necessary for valid pursuit of that goal. Following the line of authority means taking the appropriate action of the moment within the larger context of the direction one is heading.

It is not complicated; it is not obscure; by reality is meant the very simplest level of third-dimensional operationalism — what I must do in the next five minutes, for the next hour, during the next week.

It is easy to speculate and hypothesize about abstractions. It is relatively difficult to do so when action is involved: one is either on time at work or late; the beds are made or unmade; commitments are either fulfilled or our word is broken. Precision, particularly with respect to scrupulous follow-through and especially in connection with time, becomes a mighty sword to cut through the tangled Gordian knot of complicated neurotic interaction.

Neurosis hides in generalizations, in abstractions, and in unclear semantics. It is particularly fond of three areas:

God, money, and time. Because the concepts of God, money, and time are so universal and all pervasive and vague, they serve as convenient camouflage for neurotic mechanisms and are used in the service of neurotic control, manipulation of guilt, covert discharge of hostility and alleviation of inadequacy, just to mention a few.

In the Middle Ages God was the universal symbol and incorporated all other things: everything could be translated into heavenly terms. Today, in our twentieth-century civilization it is almost as though God had gone out of style in many segments of the population (a much more devastating comment than the fact that He might be dead). Today, there seems to be nothing which cannot be translated into terms of money — money being the symbol of universality at the moment.

With respect to time, all of us know how skillful timing can either produce a triumph — or contrive a disaster. The more neurotic an individual, the more skillfully he can manipulate time. Time has an elastic quality at best: chronological time may have little or no bearing on psychological time, and the knowledgeable make full use of this. "Too little and too late" is a familiar cause of failure: for want of a nail a shoe was lost, for want of a shoe the horse and then the battle and finally the war was lost — because the message arrived too late. In one's progression toward maturity and fulfillment of potential, disentangling time and money from neurosis is one of the later steps. It cannot be accomplished at all if the individual is not under authority.

The individual who is in resistance to authority can use all sorts of rationalizations or call into play any number of defensive mechanisms in order to obscure the very simple fact of what he must do. The action — each action — becomes a moment of truth, since it is either accomplished or not. And an action — any action — dispels confusion since there is an immediate and clear reading on just where things are. This is particularly true with respect to individuals who defend with passivity and then obscure with confusion.

The committed individual is never long in doubt about the reality of his situation — about what action is needed. If he does not know, he immediately moves toward finding out. Being committed to authority — the authority of reality — he is committed to performing the best (most creative, best all around, most appropriate) action. Being committed, he has no choice other than to follow the indicated correct action because commitment means that the individual will take the appropriate action, once it is pointed out to him. There are always reliable observers with whom one can check to get one's bearings; if there are none immediately apparent, they can be found.

Commitment is thus a means of shortening — actually wiping out — the time lag between perception and action; it is an emotional set or prior agreement that action be immediate once perception of its nature and direction occurs. It is in the areas of space-time — in that lag between perception and action — that neurotic mechanisms find their most fertile fields. Commitment extends action operationally to the razor's cutting edge of perception. The overriding programming on the computer is that action take place once the course is clear, and that clarity of perception occur as soon as possible. This enormously speeds up interactions and makes flexibility and change more probable.

Through all of this the role of authority is clear: the system requires that that course of action which checks out best — given all the possibilities — be carried out. The program then shifts from whether or not to act (poor Hamlet!) to the responsibility to find the best possible action. The process becomes one of progressive clarification of perception rather than an endless battle of whether or not to act. There is far less inertia in the perceptual system than in action (it is easier to see than to do); there are far fewer three-dimensional gravity drags with perception (a psychic process) than action (which involves all of the body — all bodies being subject to gravity fields).

However, increasing clarity of perception cannot occur beyond a certain point without action — or at least commitment to action. It is only in the validation of perception through action that learning and further clarification of perception can take place.

One individual can never be validly committed to another individual; one of two items of the same category can never be either superior to another or subservient to it. The only true commitment is to the line of authority and to the operational imperatives it contains. An individual can represent the line of authority, however, and it is here that much of the confusion arises. It is not to the individual but to that which he represents that the commitment is made.

Neurotic interactions do not recognize this distinction, and marriage partners with interlocking dependencies attempt to commit totally to each other, misperceiving this as the way to safeguard their own security needs. This adds validity-invalidity and false God-Devil to the neurotic equation. Actually, in "committing" to the neurotic partner, one is actually committing to oneself — displacing one's own ego into the partner and worshiping the "other half" of one's self which is actually covert narcissism and no commitment at all.

Taking appropriate action for the moment within the larger context of the direction in which one is heading — the goal — is particularly difficult when two people are in relationship and what is appropriate for one may be affected — modified or changed — by what is appropriate for the other. Actually, the goal becomes what is best all around — in the whole situation and for everyone concerned.

Critical situations arise when neurotic mechanisms are working in both individuals and neither is able to perceive the situation clearly. Thus it becomes very important that there be some sort of moderator or impartial party who has no emotional involvement in the situation and who can report clearly where he sees the neutral ground, and how best each member of the couple can reach that area in order to solve the dilemma and work through the neurotic difficulties. Of course, both partners have to be committed to maturity and growth in order for this process to work.

Eventually, when the neurotic distortions of perception have to a large measure disappeared, a couple can perform this function alone.

Pain

One of the more important aids in discovering the appropriate action — or more correctly in immediately spotting an inappropriate action — is pain. Pain serves several very important functions for individuals who want to live increasingly creative lives: it acts as warning signal, serves as evolutionary goad, and indicates dangerous reality divergence.

Pain has long been familiar as a warning signal: we pull our hand out of the fire when the pain of a burn registers; the enflamed appendix signals its dangerous state by abdominal pain. Nature has wisely built into the biological organism the protective device of pain, which acts as immediate feedback of danger — provided the system hasn't been tampered with. When the warning signal of pain occurs, the organism is given the opportunity to act in such a way as to enhance its chances for survival.

The clarity of the cause-effect warning system with respect to psychic danger is not so well-defined, probably because there is no organic mediator (as with physical pain), and also because the basic cause-and-effect mechanism (guilt) is more subject to distortion since psyches are easier to skew than cells.

The willingness to allow legitimate conscience, "the still, small voice," to be skewed out of its delicate and helpful regulatory mechanism probably arose initially from a lack of understanding of the importance and the validity of the process. Man is a pleasure-seeking animal; as such he tends to run from pain. The avoidance of pain is a very wise activity, but pain should never be avoided at the expense of silencing or blunting the mechanism for target-directed homeostasis. Nor should pain be sought for itself; it is to be felt whenever necessary as a regulatory mechanism to get us back on the track when we are off.

In the relationship of marriage, the clearer an individual's indicator and feedback mechanism, the more creative his relationship since he will know when he is off and will correct in order to be back on track as soon as possible — even before his partner calls it to his attention. With a correct "off-target" indicator, one can really become responsible for one's action. Responsibility for one's actions is one of the elements of maturity and is a very important factor in creative relationship which fulfills its potential.

There are several means by which the regulatory mechanism of psychic pain, or guilt, is blunted. One method of blunting is to silence the signal by distractions or by suppression until the sensitivity of the instrument no longer registers as soon as anything is "off target." In this case an individual with seeming impunity avoids a compelling and necessary task. The second means of blunting the instrument of regulatory feedback occurs with over-conditioning toward guilt. This occurs in mild cases in families with too high expectation levels or guilt-producing religious standards (or both), in moderate to severe cases in perfection-demanding and guilt-imposing families; and in cases of pathology with schizophrenic or schizophrenic-producing family members. In any case, children are made to feel responsible for and guilty about almost anything and everything. Responses tailored to deal with this overwhelming guilt become neurotic patterns and defective character structure up to the point of actual psychotic breaks with reality.

The third stimulus toward neurotic guilt is found in the deification of martyrdom inherent in the sadomasochistic elements of western civilization. Martyrdom assigns the highest value to death rather than to fulfillment, not only with respect to religion, but also with respect to love — as with Tristan and Isolde, Héloïse and Abélard, Romeo and Juliet, and many others. Actually, self-sacrifice is only legitimate when no fundamental aspect of the self is sacrificed. There can be no creative fulfilled relationship (marriage or other) where martyrdom is involved.

It is one of the tasks of the maturing human being to strip off the layers of false guilt so that the delicate flame of awareness of what is appropriate action can operate freely. "Appropriate" is a far more apt word than "right," which implies a moral judgment. There is no necessity to assign moral values to an action which either leads to an individual's more optimal functioning or does not; questions of right and wrong merely complicate what should be straightforward regulatory feedback mechanisms of more or less efficient, more or less goal oriented, and so on.

Operationally, it has always been found wise — both in personal life and in the guiding of a patient — to work toward the elimination of guilts which arise from present life circumstances. There are a number of simple techniques for this of which the following are important samples: no commitment should be made unless it can be carried out; schedules or sequences of action which are capable of fulfillment are made progressively so that in the course of time, all those actions which the individual needs to take are taken as he becomes capable of managing them; all tasks which are begun must be completed or a more satisfactory action determined and taken; no promise should be made unless it can be fulfilled (a process which will lead gradually to complete integrity of the person with respect to action or words).

As these suggestions are incorporated into everyday life, present time or current guilt is whittled down and eliminated. The individual is then able to deal with past time confusions, incorrect conditioning, and cultural biases with respect to guilt and value judgments. Also, couples are able to proceed to deeper relationship problems only when everyday actions are corrected as far as possible. It is impossible for the reality feedback mechanism (clear conscience) to operate when it is obscured by neurotic guilt; it is impossible to separate out neurotic guilt until the individual is as free as possible from current guilt which always overlies and intertwines and obscures neurotic guilt.

The accurate feedback of non-neurotic guilt is very important to any close relationship, and is essential to a committed relationship of growth. Before neurotic guilt can be dealt with, everyday guilts of commission and omission must be eliminated as far as is possible. Pain (the pain of guilt) is the mechanism by which the needle registers that something is not functioning correctly: whether there is imminent danger, or we are off target.

The other functions of pain — as evolutionary goad and signal of dangerous reality divergence — are not widely recognized; they appear to be associated in some form with maturation and man's evolutionary path. It seems important to note these functions because of our concern with committed couples moving toward fulfillment of their own potential.

The pain that is a spur to growth is familiar to us. We can feel this by pausing for a moment and pondering on any undeveloped ability of ours which we have been considering doing something about — but haven't. All of us have known the sharp prick of a goad from that Spanish we didn't study before going to Mexico or that painting class we really wanted to take but didn't; the recipe we didn't try or the invention we didn't pursue. It almost seems as though life keeps after us along our path, jabbing little spurs into us when we tarry unnecessarily or take the wrong turning. The function of this pain and the process by which it works need not be elaborated on.

The more painful signal of divergence between potential and achievement is usually camouflaged since this divergence rests so close to the site of inadequacy that one can afford to feel such pain fully only if already committed to the pathway of change. An individual need only to think of what he wanted most to be when there were no limits on his horizon and to compare that with his location at the moment in order to feel a twinge of this pain. Or, if he can peel back the calluses covering the times of decision toward action when the action was not taken, then the pain of divergence between perception and action can be felt.

One of the most fatal errors that we can make is the failure to act according to our perceptions. When we do not act as we perceive is "best" (with no moral implication) for us to act, then that default of action dulls succeeding perception. The continuing refusal to act on the basis of perception results in the gradual loss of perception until one becomes psychically blind, thus moving over into the area of real pathology.

In real pathology, the cause-and-effect mechanism is shifted, displacing the point where pain is felt into another area and obscuring the origin of the difficulty. Through suppression, repression, and anesthesia, the pain is disconnected from the stimulus which aroused it and the stimulus is repressed, along with the feeling of the pain itself, and there is displacement or projection of the feeling. The anesthesia of the pain (and repression and projection) blocks awareness of the process.

When pain is submerged, suppressed, repressed or anesthetized and projected, it obviously cannot act as a corrective mechanism. If only we could discover how this anesthesia projection is mediated at the cellular level and reverse the process, our most recalcitrant psychiatric illnesses might become amenable to treatment. However, it is apparent that if there is any suppression, repression, anesthetizing or skewing of pain in any way, the problem which it is signaling not only cannot be solved — it won't even be recognized. Marriage does not thrive — in fact it cannot survive — on nonrecognition of problems.

In a society which is becoming progressively dedicated to the pursuit of the pleasure principle, a healthy respect for pain — a willingness to examine its functions, and a commitment to move toward its astringent clarification — will effect a deep change in the individual involved. If enough individuals are involved, perhaps there might be a deep change in mankind, with a possible avoidance of the disappearance of the species. In any case, for each individual who changes, there is progressive movement toward fulfillment of the potential within himself and of the potential of any relationship in which he is involved.

11

The Sacrament of Sex

Parameters of Successful Sex

ACTUALLY the whole question of sex is a paradox. On the one hand it is a snicker subject, bastard of Victorian-Puritan suppression by means of the submerged half of mankind which is typified by four-letter words scrawled on outhouse walls. On the other hand it is the stimulus which most bombards our eyes, ears, and sensibilities in written, printed, or flickering-screen word. In addition, mores and morals are changing so fast that the acceptable sex practice a parent describes to his son or daughter at dinner may be outmoded by breakfast.

To some people sexual intercourse is a pleasant titillation, comparable to a glass of wine with dinner; to others it is an onerous task or a painful horror; to many it is the total refreshment of a fulfilled experience of integration; while to most it is a pleasure — varied and varying — but puzzling and unpredictable. What is even more difficult to understand is that sexual experience can run the gamut from chilling repugnance and sadistic destructiveness to the heights of the unitive — sometimes even with the same couple.

Generalization about sexual interaction is difficult, if not impossible. Sex covers the feeling spectrum as though a kaleidoscope of all the rainbow. With pleasure-pain it ranges from agony to the transcendental and can include the emptiness of non-feeling. It can be in time, out of time, or beyond time — past, present, or future time; and it can include all space or none, any dimension or all dimensions or no dimension at all.

How is it that this one phenomenon of human interaction can be so much and so little and so varied?

Man is a sensual animal: his basic experience comes to him by means of his five senses. Anything which leaves out the body leaves out an integral part of any human experience. Since we are all sensing animals, the primary source of our experience is in our bodies with all of their vibrating sensory receptors. Our experiences are not only "felt" as pain, pleasure, warmth, pressure, sight, smell, taste, and touch, but they are registered in our brain in a matrix of past experiences and associational frameworks which we have learned to call thinking and feeling.

For purposes of discussion, we divide ourselves into mind, body, and psyche (emotions or feeling), although we can no more divide mind from body than we can separate the yolk from the white of egg — before breaking the shell. Thus to the basic unit of body, with all of its sensitivities to a number of dimensions of feelings, we must add the full spectrum of emotional range and a huge computer bank of past experiences, associations, and combinations of all these which we call thoughts and attitudes. Thoughts, feelings, and attitudes are further arranged into patterns which we label personality, temperament, and character. The interaction among all of the elements contains so many possible combinations and permutations that the mind is staggered just to conceptualize them. This infinity of possible interactions gives human experience vast range and richness.

We must not forget, however, that the basic experiencing unit is the body, despite man's attempts, through church, state, and literature, to deify or romanticize sex into the sole realm of mind or spirit. It is in a body that the experience originates, and it is the body we must first consider with respect to sex. It seems foolish or redundant to remind ourselves that one's body must be alive and vibrant — healthy — in order for sex to be experienced properly. A tired or sick body, a debilitated body, a degenerate body, will experience only within the limits of its constrictions.

Further, rewarding sexuality is not possible any more than is rewarding sensuality for anyone who feels that his body is dirty, carnal, or of a lower order or category than his mind or spirit. The false and unfortunate dichotomy between mind and body seems to have appeared in conjunction with Judeo-Christian civilization and was given a healthy kick toward longevity by the Puritans and then the Victorians. The separation of mind from body (or of intellect from feeling) is not only inaccurate and misleading, but it enhances the already too pervasive concept of duality which is so destructive to both individual man and collective mankind. Duality fragments man; his fulfillment lies in unity.

Fulfilling sex is the most available means we have to lead us to a unitive experience. As we touched on briefly with beginning sexual experiences, sexual interaction should cover the whole rainbow panorama of feeling and sensuality; it should include the transcendence of duality; and in the fullest experiences of integration it should include the mystic experience of cosmic unity where some form of ultimate reality becomes a concomitant and intermeshing force.

But we cannot think our way into sex; nor can we always feel with our senses or feel with our emotions into it. And once there, it isn't always fulfilling. Why? Or why not?

In order to experience fulfilling sex, there are several parameters which must be satisfied. The first and foremost is love. There must ideally be love (and passion) or, failing love, there must be mutual affection and regard between two individuals.

What is love — that elusive emotion celebrated by poets and described in as many ways as there are words? Is it some magic emotion, some elixir of feeling which is stumbled on by chance or luck? Is it some special chemistry which occurs between two people which is available only to certain chosen ones and not to others?

Love can be any of this; it can be all of this and much more. Each individual probably experiences it differently, and it is considered all things to all people. However, in its simplest essence, love is actually the absence of barriers.

To the extent to which barriers are in abeyance, to that extent will an individual feel deeply at one with himself, with his loved one, and with the world. The implication is that when in love an individual is at one with all of his environment — a state which is impossible unless he is at one with himself.

This absence of barriers — and let us be very clear that it is not just loss of inhibitions or letting go of controls (although both are included) — is the precondition for what we call love, or for any unitary or mystic experience. Situational factors of the moment — physiological, environmental, psychic, relationship — give flavor, direction, and extent to the experience, and determine what aspects of feeling and levels of consciousness will be involved, and how it is perceived by the individuals who are experiencing it.

The absence of barriers is most possible when there is deep feeling and affection between two people. The most likely occurrence of this absence of barriers is with two mutually attracted individuals who are committed to each other and who are walking together on the same path toward the same goal of self-fulfillment.

However, there may also be a sudden abeyance of barriers between two recently met individuals who unexpectedly find themselves in deep communion. It is important to recognize the possibility of this flowering-into-relationship without the continuity of past time and without the necessity for continuing relationship. The existence of this possibility is an insight into the quality of Nowness which permeates all of unitive experience. Actually, the core of the mystic or unitive experience is outside of time; it transcends space-time.

The unitive experience, either alone or shared, can exist with or without sexual intercourse. However, one of its highest expressions, despite the words of many churches to the contrary, occurs between two individuals who are in love, who are committed to themselves, to each other, and to life — and who mesh on many levels. We shall have more to say on meshing later.

Besides love — the absence of barriers — there are two

more factors which are vital to fulfilling sex: commitment; and letting go of controls. One cannot experience beyond time — the important element of the transcendental experience — unless one can let go of barriers. One cannot let go of barriers if one cannot trust. One cannot trust if there is not commitment to something beyond the self and some experience that life is capable of being trusted.

It is in the letting go of controls — in the abandoning of oneself to whatever comes — that the miracle of orgasm, of fusion, and of transcendental and unitive experience can occur.

This is specifically and particularly true with respect to sexual experience: one must be committed to allowing whatever may come; one must totally abandon oneself to the experience of the moment — allowing the experience to change from moment to moment so that whatever nuances and levels are possible will come into being. This letting go to whatever may come also helps one go beyond any unconscious barriers against physical expression of intimacy.

Since man is a sensual animal, the input from his five senses forms the basis of his experience. Sensory stimuli impinge and are immediately "felt"; there is no putting off until tomorrow the pinprick of today; nor can the happiness of the moment be bottled as medicine against the gloom of next week.

The more an individual accepts his body, the more he or she can enjoy the warmth of closeness, the play of the tactile over skin surfaces, the stimulation of erogenous zones and the heat of passion. The greater the stimulation the more the individual will revel in feelings of sensuality and sexuality, and the more varied and intense will be the total experience. After all, our bodies are the "temple" of our existence in third-dimensional reality.

Often our bodies know far better than we do. They are sometimes drawn together involuntarily (and as though inevitably) when there may be no apparent meshing of minds or psyches, settling in together as though they are two parts of a whole which have finally been joined. If minds and emotions fail to mesh, along with the bodies, the relationship will be a difficult one to maintain: either it will remain on a superficial emotional level but with deep physical meshing and passion and much pulling together and pulling apart; or the strength of the physical attraction of the two bodies will hold the couple together until apparent differences have been reconciled and growth takes place in the couple toward mutual compatibility and real companionship.

The almost cellular attraction of two bodies for each other so that with intercourse they fuse and seem indissoluble is fascinating and leads to speculation as to whether the meshing arises from some racial necessity, some attraction from past or future time, or some evolutionary purpose whereby individuals who ordinarily would not be attracted to each other are drawn together to enhance racial variation or to work out disparities which otherwise would never be subject to change. In these cases of strong attraction, the extent of body trust between the two individuals (despite how untrusting or uncomprehending the minds) is almost a palpable reality. This is the same whether the individuals who seem very different are drawn together in a casual relationship which will go no further in depth or growth, or whether the physical drawing together initiates a deeply meaning-ful and long-lasting relationship — possible only after a great deal of hard work on both parts. The interesting element is the strong attraction of the two bodies, al-most to the point of cellular magnetism.

Just as there are intelligences of the mind and of the emotions (intuition), there is undoubtedly cellular intel-ligence (as with instinct in animals), which may well be the wisest of all of the intelligences with respect to the overall state of the organism. Its messages are difficult to read. Just as the genetic code was suspected long before the discovery of DNA and RNA, the intuitions of cellu-lar intelligence in human beings have manifested them-selves before we have accurate knowledge of a possible site or of how the mechanism might work. Certainly racial history must to some extent be transmitted in the genes just as is the individual's biological ancestry — racial history in the sense of the psychological (the accumulated wisdom of mankind in what Jung called the collective unconscious). It may even be that all of the accumulated experience and wisdom of mankind — and maybe of all creation — is available at some level of consciousness or other dimension only waiting for man to tap into. This area might be called a place of all knowledge. Reported experiences of individuals while in altered states of con-sciousness (whether through illness, religious trance, drugs, or ecstasy) often indicate something of this nature. It might well be worth man's while to send some probes inward into this area as well as outward into space; he might learn faster and more safely from inner dis-covery than he does from the highly emphasized outer exploration.

However, for our purposes, we need only note that there is probably an intelligence which arises from and is specific to the cellular structure just as there is an intelligence of the mind and of the emotions. Operationally, one should be open to intuitions from any source, and when the organism is in a state of integrated unity, certainly all of the intelligences must be in line with each other and with reality.

It is interesting to speculate about the strong attraction of two individuals for each other and whether this pull of cell to cell and body to body and the resulting fusion represents something out of past time which has been lived through in unity, or whether it is a pull to effect growth changes in two individuals who belong on some sort of path together but do not recognize each other because of the disparity of their experience and backgrounds. Certainly we do know that in those growth-union-marriages which are for the rest of life, this bodily drawing together into fusion is a very strong element.

But we have wandered far afield from our consideration of the parameters of sex.

Besides being a vehicle for love and a means of expressing a spectrum of variegated emotions, the act of sexual intercourse is one of the most delicate indicators known: it is a reflection of the short-term and the long-term state of each of the individuals and also of their interaction; and there is immediate revelation of whether anything alien to sexual feelings is present.

Sexual interaction is a barometer of conflict, within oneself and with others (internal or external), and a thermometer of barriers, blocks, and unresolved problems. It is a complete and thorough statement about the ability to let go of the controls and to trust another human being — and also a diagram of the unity within each individual and in their interaction. And if a person is suffering from a disparity between his potential and his achievement, the discrepancy will be reflected in his sexual experience.

As surely as mercury records the degree of heat, the act of love registers any barriers which secretly exist within us. Just as moods reflect themselves in willingness to approach (or desire to avoid) a loved one, inner restrictions and barriers to another human being (and to the state of openness) reveal themselves as impediments to the full experience of love. This barometer-thermometer of sexual interaction is a very valuable tool in helping uncover obstacles toward relationship and growth.

The use of sexual interaction as a means for expression of other emotions immediately imposes a further limitation: nothing can ride on sex and still allow the fullness of the experience to come into being. To the extent that an individual wishes adequacy or power, or control, or the discharge of hostility, more than mutual satisfaction (and attempts consciously or unconsciously to express this desire in intercourse), to that extent will feelings and experience be inhibited — up to the point of nonoccurrence.

All of us are familiar with wives who give their husbands the come-on, with sexy look or loving squeeze, only to develop a raging headache just when their husbands are ready to take them to bed; we have all seen husbands who pay court to every other woman at a party and then wax exceedingly wroth when their wives don't reward them with passionate kisses when they are alone. If Daniel comes home frustrated from work and insists night after night that Helena make love to him in order to alleviate his own inner feelings of inadequacy, Helena will soon cool to his apparent ardor. If Consuela butters up Samuel with a lush meal and lusher promises for the evening, he is not likely to react kindly to her ensuing request for a mink coat.

Unfortunately, two areas of critical importance to man — food as well as sex — are most commonly abused in games of power and one-upmanship. An infinity of means and mechanisms could be catalogued whereby negative or "unacceptable" feelings are expressed as an accompaniment to these two activities which should be involved only with basic nourishment and refreshment for individuals. The few examples given above are un-complicated ones of sex being used in the service of other feelings such as hostility, inadequacy or control. There is an infinity of possible variations.

As has been mentioned several times before, noth-ing can ride on sexuality without inhibiting and limiting it. Any restriction or constraint, individual or societal, limits the experiencing of sexuality; neurotic mechanisms interfere with its free functioning; and sexual interaction is diminished by any internal or external problem unless one can let go so completely that the barriers and difficul-ties are temporarily in abeyance.

One of the values of the sacrament of sex (because sacrament it is) is as an indicator of these barriers, as a locater of their nature and site, and as a means of working through these problems when discovered.

Barriers to Sex: Lack of Feeling and Inadequacy
It is interesting that any major problem which arises in sexual interaction — outside of traumatic sexual experi-ences in youth — is almost without fail a problem of

defect of feeling or of adequacy — not of sex. Contrary to general available information the most important site for the opening of sexuality lies not in the genitals but in the solar plexus, which appears to be the focus of most of our emotions. If that area can be opened so that feelings flow between partners, sexuality is bound to follow.

Sometimes the question is one of draining off limitations, inhibitions, and loadings. Methods can be cultivated for "letting go" at the time and for working on the problem at other times. These methods fall into the realm of the therapeutic, and include techniques used by sensitivity groups, psychodrama, experiencing the Now, acting "as if," and so on, as well as symbolic or fantasy-type methods. An imaginative individual can visualize a spigot where the solar plexus lies (in that area from the lower part of the breastbone down to the navel). Once the spigot is "felt," he can turn it on and let all the negative feelings and difficulties flow out. As the area clears, he is amazed to feel the pressure and weight lessening, and finally the flow of feelings beginning between himself and his mate.

This flow is enhanced if the couple stand or lie facing each other, closely touching the length of their bodies, especially close in the solar plexus areas. Once one individual is open to the flow of feelings, the other is usually carried along into openness, and both develop feelings of affection, warmth, and love — with sexuality following closely behind.

Although frigid women have sexuality cut off from feeling, it is usually the man who doesn't really feel. It is as though, in our society, men are allowed two feelings: hostility and sexuality. Women are allowed the gentle emotions of warmth, tenderness and affection. This is a phenomenon which is not usually recognized, let alone understood. Since men use the same words women do about feeling, and since they *think* they feel and *speak* as though they feel (not knowing themselves that something is lacking), it is very difficult for them to know that they do not feel. It is much the same as with a color-blind person before he discovers his difficulty: he has names for the colors red and green and discriminates between the two in his perceptions. However, he is perceiving shades of gray and brown, not red as it exists distinct from green.

Actually, almost all men in our culture have a deficit of feeling to some extent: it is greater in professional men (accountants, lawyers and doctors, particularly surgeons) than in artists, and seems to be greatest of all in mechanical engineers. It is only as one observes the miracle of the birth of feeling that the picture begins to clarify, both for the man who feels, and for the observer.

The causes for this cutoff of feeling are probably twofold: first, the rigid cultural differentiation which allows little girls to feel and to cry freely but requires that boys suppress all forms of "sissy" feelings; and the cutting off of feeling very early in a sensitive child because of too much pain. In engineers one sees sensitive men who had so much emotional pain and confusion when they were young that they not only shut off feelings but carried the process even further by moving away from people and toward things in their vocation in order to make doubly sure they would not be further hurt.

The lack of feeling areas of emotion — the stronger

emotions for a woman, the gentler for a man — puts a limitation on sexual experiencing. One of the important functions which modern men and women can perform for each other is to widen their partner's capacity to feel. The man helps the woman open to her feelings of sexuality and aggressiveness and to allow them fully. She is much more conditioned against sex than he: if for two decades one must say, "No, no, a thousand times no!" it is difficult to suddenly reverse the programming and say, "Yes!" The woman in turn teaches the man the value of tenderness and sensitivity and how the gentle emotions can act to embellish even strong passion.

There are other specific techniques which help bring feeling. A very simple one is the movement of hands over the body of the partner, not just the erogenous zones, but the whole body so that tactile feelings come into play. This might start with a massage or back rub of the one who feels cut off, moving at times into breast and genital areas and away again so that sexuality is subtly brought into play.

It is interesting to consider the semantic link between "to feel" as in tactile and "to feel" emotionally. Even the word emotion comes from *ex* (out of) and *movere* (to move): arising out of, or from motion, or moving out from. It is quite possible that adults who are too restricted in their feelings were prevented as children from moving and feeling freely in their environment and thus suffered from too early a constraint of exploratory and mastery urges. They were probably not allowed to "touch" bodies — their own or others — or probably even (valuable?) objects; they were certainly not allowed to feel whenever and whatever they wanted, and it is quite possible that when they reached out for new experiences and for learning about things by touching them and putting them into their mouths, their hands were slapped. The fear of having fingers or hands chopped off may very well be as serious a castration worry as the fear of loss of a penis and would be a source of restriction for girls as well as for boys.

While we are discussing aids to the feeling of sexuality, we should not overlook some of the obvious means available to any couple. In the first place, the constant orientation should be toward opening up sexually: both individuals should move toward sexual feelings at any and every (appropriate) opportunity. If listening to music together opens them to each other and to sex, they should plan for music, maybe even making love to special pieces; if dancing is of benefit, they should have a time of rocking and rolling together before maybe indulging in a double striptease as they go to bed. If reading poetry or erotic passages enhances feeling, that should be done; romantic movies often stimulate and awaken sexual desire, and so forth.

Each individual and every couple has different likes and dislikes; various stimuli make them more open to each other and to sexual feelings. These different aids should be assiduously sought out and cultivated so they can be used to help the couple toward greater openness and feelings.

Selective and careful drinking can be of great benefit for those who have no reservations about alcohol and whose barriers lower with a drink or two. Care must be taken against too much liquor (which varies among individuals and with conditions) because even a little bit too much blurs feelings, allows negative elements from the unconscious to be expressed, and depresses rather than relaxes.

Also, the man should not be afraid to use force judiciously in his lovemaking. Many women at heart want to be overwhelmed and carried away into passionate feelings. However, there is a very delicate line, as no woman wants to be forced against her "real" will; nor does a normal woman want to be hurt in lovemaking beyond the love bites or strawberry bruises which enhance passion and are not even felt as pain during strong sexual interaction. The distinction between rape and force is the discriminating line: it should be the force of strength which is applied in the lovemaking and not the force of imposition of action against the will of the other person.

There is also another technique which has been found to be very effective in arousing sexual feelings in both men and women and has served as a valuable tool against impotence: nursing. It may sound strange to consider having a man "nurse" at his wife's breast; however, it works relatively rapidly and in almost every case arouses both the husband and the wife. It is as though the man goes back to get some basic nourishment which he failed to receive in childhood (some men swear that they can taste milk coming from their wives and that when the technique is successful they feel wonderfully full of milk, deliciously satisfied, and sexually aroused); at the same time, the woman has great feelings of adequacy at providing "nourishment" for the man she loves.

Breasts are highly erogenous zones; any stimulation of them should be arousing, but nursing appears to be especially so. Also, sexual feelings while a mother is nursing her child are universal; if they are not felt the chances are that the mother is frightened of her sexuality toward her child and blocks the feelings from her awareness. The nursing technique taps into this process.

The progression of a man from sexual immaturity and impotence has been observed in patients merely by means of the addition of a nursing "schedule" of ten to fifteen minutes night and morning, with any resulting sexual feelings carried through to completion.

Psychological impotence (and "immature" penis and "immature sexuality" which all appear to be different forms of the same phenomenon) arises from fear or hostility or a combination of the two. Probably a large component of the "immaturity" contains unaccepted and unacceptable animal and so-called sadistic elements of the man's feelings, a combination of hostility and un-resolved oral dependency (experienced as the desire to bite that which one loves) and fear of betraying himself in giving any indication of the presence of these feelings. Suppression of any element of strong feeling supresses sexuality itself. The man chooses to appear immature and undeveloped rather than to reveal such "dangerous" feelings.

Hostility (often unconscious) on the part of either the man *or the woman* can result in the inability to achieve and maintain an erection. Hostility on the part of the man can be from feeling that he is expected to do too much or that his body processes are under control of the woman, or from invalidly imposed guilt about sexuality. The fear can arise because of strict childhood repression of any show of sexuality, from fear of being caught mastur-bating, fear of having an erection (which haunts a pubescent boy's days, particularly in school situations), fear of inadequacy and nonperformance, and so on.

The technique of nursing takes the husband and wife back to the most basic situation of nourishment, and redoes it while both allowing and rewarding sexual feelings. The "child" has the experience of relearning that there *is* enough to nourish him and that he *will* get his share, and — almost more important in our situation — that he will not only be allowed body feelings by mother, but that she will feel these feelings with him, and will help him to fulfillment and nourishment in *both* of the two basic areas of food and sex.

At the same time a couple is using nursing as a technique to open sexuality and to overcome feelings of inadequacy and impotence, there should be some sort of regular daily hostility discharge for both of them. Hostility must be separated out from sexuality; as it begins to separate, the need for a discharge mechanism arises. There are a number of therapeutic techniques for this: punching bag for the man (not a speed bag, rather a canvas or duffel bag filled with torn newspapers), pounding a couch or bed for the woman; throwing "tantrums" on the bed when alone for both; smashing up cardboard cartons; and throwing clay (and then working it with the hands) among others.

Getting the hostility out by direct fighting of the couple is not recommended. When fights start (and they will inevitably arise during this period of working through old and uncreative neurotic patterns), the couple should immediately separate and write down, each of them, the events which led up to the difficulty. These "reports" should be gone over together simultaneously with either a professional counselor or a very competent "referee" so that the mechanics of each individual's difficulty become clear to them both. Half the battle — provided, of course, that the couple want to solve the problem — is in making unconscious neurotic mechanisms conscious and overt. If the true desire is to maintain the interlocking neurosis while verbal noises are made about wanting to solve the problem, this will very soon become apparent to an objective third party. The couple should then be helped to see what it is they really want, and how to go about relieving the situation of unrealistic pseudo-desires so that they can move directly toward achieving their goal, no matter how neurotic (so long as it is not harmful to either), in order that they may see how the achievement of the goal feels, and find out if that is really what they want.

If the avowed goal is sexuality but the real goal is control, this will become evident as overt mechanisms are initiated to move toward the sexuality, discharging hostility and unraveling conflict along the way. Then the real problem of wanting to control more than wanting to relate or to experience sexuality can be dealt with and hopefully brought to resolution. It is impossible, however, to solve any problem of sexuality when sexuality is not the problem but merely a reflection of it.

The other major barrier to full expression of sex is the feeling of inadequacy.

Deep at the core of any difficulty in human relationship — and especially in sex — lies inadequacy. Because feelings of inadequacy generate such agonizing pain, we barricade them off and camouflage the hiding place with all sorts of defensive protection.

Unfortunately, that doesn't solve the problem. Our elusive ghost slips out in the dark of night to find relief in expressing itself wherever possible and turns up in the very activities we are engaged in in order to get rid of it. What kind of relationship can a man or woman have who seeks to find potency and masculinity (or femininity) as an escape from inadequacy at home or at work? What kind of sexual satisfaction will result from an affair (or promiscuity) which was entered into as a means of avoiding the inadequacy of the marital bed?

If the individual's inadequacy is of long duration and has taproots in the earliest imposition of controls on bodily functions, the need to control will be more powerful than the immediate capacity for love. Much female frigidity, as well as its male counterpart of difficulty in letting go and ejaculating, has its genesis in the too early attempt to control urinary and bowel functions — at the demand of parents or other authorities — before there was actual biological and developmental capacity for the control which was demanded.

The capacity for voluntary regulation of urinary and bowel functions develops somewhere within the second to fourth years of life in a girl but not until the third to fifth years in a boy. Why a boy's development occurs at a slower rate than a girl's is one of those puzzling questions which nature has given us to solve. We can speculate about whether there is something which develops at a slower pace in more movement-oriented male bodies; or if it is possible that the female of the species had to be grown up and ready to reproduce earlier than the male for racial reasons. Whatever the original design, it must be very clearly understood — and taken into account — that up to adolescence boys mature more slowly than girls on almost all fronts, and maturity is usually demanded by unknowing parents before even girls are capable of achieving it. This makes the demands on later-maturing boys that much more stringent and punishing, particularly in terms of feelings of inadequacy.

Control of body functions is demanded by parents (unless they are very relaxed or had the good fortune to be familiar with child care practices like those of Dr. Spock) long before either girls or boys are capable. This incapacity through immaturity probably has to do with the pattern of progressive insulation of nerve pathways in the brain. Without insulation, reliable and consistent control is impossible. The demand for complete continence at night is a particularly impossible demand for any child under the five to seven age range, and many boys — still within normal range — take even longer.

Sigmund Freud correctly saw the importance of the anal level of development in character patterns of independence, giving, and relationship to authority — and the neurotic consequences of the incomplete negotiation of this level of development. However, he seems to have overlooked the equal importance of the urinary controls, particularly important because sexual organs are in such close proximity to the urinary, even overlapping in boys. Early generalization of the too stringent necessity for control can have disastrous consequences in adult incapacity to let go sexually. It becomes quite a therapeutic task to separate out the various functions and free the "letting go" controls from invalid restraints.

A further difficulty, particularly with boys, can arise from its usually being mother, or a female member of the household, who has insisted that the boy control himself and that he withhold or produce urine and feces on demand. The child is made to feel inadequate because of his incapacity to control, although the fault is not of his own doing; he is forced to produce at certain times and places and under time restrictions; he is forbidden body exploration, particularly sexual and especially masturbation; and he is ridiculed, punished, and rejected for not conforming. Small wonder that the child feels that adults (particularly his mother) want to possess his body and control it totally along with its production. At the same time, he intuitively knows that the control of body functions rightfully belongs only to the person himself.

If the pressure is severe enough on the child, in addition to the feelings of inadequacy which are grafted into his body, he will become hostile over the excessive expectations and will react in whatever way he can manage — by not controlling, by withholding and overcontrolling, by temper tantrums, or by going passive and refusing to do anything at all. With the refusal to act at all he sets himself up for failure by not doing those things which are right for him. This warping of the whole mechanism of cause-and-effect distorts cooperation, production (and thus achievement and creativity), and relationship with others (especially those in authority).

This whole syndrome sets in self-defeating patterns of reactions *against* authority rather than *to* a stimulus, which conditions the child in non-achieving. If the child gets more attention by his withholding and non-achieving than he does by doing the things that are best for himself, he early acquires neurotic patterns of failure and nonfulfillment of potential, the "loser syndrome." The whole situation is further complicated by the fact that children are dependent on the adults in their environ-ment. Consequently dependency, hostility, rebellion against authority, and non-achievement (even self-de-structiveness) become one tangled mass.

If the situation is severe, passive resistance becomes a way of life or at least the usual response to stress; with pathology, the passive resistance ends up as actual im-mobilization and withdrawal. The child refuses to move at all, literally, and is not amenable to normal techniques of relationship or learning. In order to survive in such a situation he develops a skewed perception of reality; at some level inside his head his own passivity is mistakenly equated with invulnerability (I've won over the adults; they can't make me talk or move), which becomes omnip-otence (I can win out over everybody; I control the whole world by my refusal to move or act). The child feels himself above the rules and impervious to them as with psychopaths, or he will retreat into his own world where he has complete control but becomes schizophrenic, the direction being determined by genetic factors and other relationship elements in his environment.

Withdrawal and refusal to come to terms with reality — and with the measuring stick of reality which we call cause-and-effect — are actions contrary to life; they are oriented toward destruction and death rather than toward living and creativity. The child who learns withdrawal and passivity and refuses to come to terms with reality may early develop a death wish which manifests itself minimally in a refusal to produce and achieve and fulfill himself, but maximally in suicidal tendencies.

Passivity is one of the great antagonists of creative sex; nothing can happen when two blobs sit there waiting for someone else to do something for them. Further, creative relationship is not really possible under conditions where one or both members are biasing reality to their own unconscious needs for inactivity, omnipotence, and winning out over authority.

It is easy to understand how a child who has been conditioned to defend against a mother who demanded control of everything, even body functions, will have vigorous defenses against letting any woman close to him. He is even less able to let down his barriers and relax controls in a feeling interaction with a woman. Obviously when the unconscious game is to defeat momma, the wife who is in relationship with this child-grown-to-manhood will suffer much frustration and unhappiness, particularly in sexual relations.

Under conditions where such neurotic binds are operating, sex becomes an automatic or at least an unfeeling act — if indeed it can be performed without the false aids of fantasy, fetishes, and rituals, or even performed at all. Impotence, premature ejaculation, frigidity (in men lack of ability to have an ejaculation) all find their genesis in the early years and the child's reactions to the complicated environment in which he found himself (with very important emphasis on his gaining control of his body and learning to use it) and his attempt to survive psychically.

Society adds further burdens and taboos, conditioning boys away from the tender emotions while they grow into men. As we have seen, only girls are allowed to cry and be gentle and soft; boys are assigned the areas of sexuality, drive, and aggression (all too often combined with hostility) as their permissible fields of operation. On this scene the Age of Reason sheds its light so that intellect, logic and rationality are given the highest values in the hierarchy while feeling and irrationality, both fundamentally important for sexual expresssion and love, are assigned to the weak (women and children) and to the lowest values in our particular culture.

Actually, it is probably remarkable that as many people have as successful experience in sexual relations as they do; it is a real tribute to nature's basic design capacity.

However, our sexual experiences aren't good enough, and most couples know it. Certainly the frenetic pressure observable on all sides toward the sexual and the explosion of formerly unacceptable sexual practices into widely pursued activities demonstrate that mankind hasn't found what he is looking for — and that there is a lot of steam behind the search, and behind the insistence on finding something better, one way or another.

In the meantime, is there anything that can be done about feelings of inadequacy?

Inadequacy arises from many sources; there is very little we can do to work directly on most of them. Often the feelings of inadequacy do not reflect real areas of disability; they are just feelings of lack and inferiority on the part of the person. Such basic feelings of inadequacy are overcome only with maturational changes of the individual and movement toward his own fulfillment. However, there are a few prophylactic actions one can take with respect to feelings of inadequacy: one can stay guilt free in everyday life; and one can practice self-discipline.

There is no more immediate agitator of inadequacy feelings than not completing the tasks which we set for ourselves. If I make the statement that I am going to walk over and open the door, and I don't do it (I forget, I am distracted, I balk), I have had a strong lesson in the fact that I cannot depend on myself. There is nothing which makes one feel more helpless and inadequate than the knowledge that he cannot depend on himself. Yet every instance wherein we fail to follow through with self-discipline adds to our feeling of not being able to depend on ourselves.

Therefore, just as with guilt, one must follow through: commitments must not be made which cannot be fulfilled; tasks should not be undertaken which cannot be completed; our word must never be given when it cannot be kept. Every time we let ourselves down we add another drop to the poison of inadequacy inside ourselves; every time we follow through we neutralize a drop of poison.

With respect to commitments, it is important to separate expectations from the actuality of what must be done. The shoulds, the oughts, and the musts are mostly neurotic remnants from earlier years and have very little operational validity in our lives except to keep us feeling constantly inadequate and guilty because we cannot fulfill them. Actually, many of them are unverbalized and most are unconscious.

A very simple mechanism for handling the discrimination between what we (or others) think we should do, and that which we need to do is to keep two lists. On the first list everything should be written down that we think we must, ought, should, could, want to do. That probably should be a large piece of paper, and items should be added whenever they come to mind. The second list can be a small spiral notebook in which we list *each day* those tasks which we are going to do that day, the last task being a check of the checklist to see that everything has been completed. Nothing should ever be put on this list which is not going to be done; and as each task is completed, it is checked off. Tasks from the larger list can be moved to the smaller one if and when appropriate. The value of the two lists is that one is a record of all kinds of things, mostly unrealistic and perhaps years away; the other is an operational list *tied down by time* of what we are actually going to do that day. This helps us separate neurotic demands and over-expectations from that which we can actually do to order and discipline our lives.

It is startling what a difference the institution of self-discipline will make in our feelings about ourselves and in the order of our lives and in our relations with each other. It is also amazing what immediate and positive changes the institution of absolute fulfillment of commitments can make. When we become reliable we can trust ourselves. When we trust ourselves then we can proceed to trust others. And only with trust can we let go so that we can feel freely.

Timing and Orgasm

As has been mentioned earlier, sexual satisfaction — for one's partner and for one's self — is a skill, and an artistic one at that. Just as with any other skill, it can be acquired with practice, and then further embellished with myriads of variations. There must be openness, lack of barriers, meshing of two individuals, and sensitivity to one another's needs — which knowledge and experience help bring — and there must be experiential knowledge of one's own body and of the body of one's mate. These are necessary, along with the willingness to experiment and the desire that someone we love feel deeply. Toward this purpose one should be willing to hold off for oneself temporarily or to speed up the timing so that the experience can be mutual.

Timing is a very important element in sexuality and can come *only* with experience. Even with someone one loves deeply and who is committed to the same goals we are, it takes three or four months of adjustment before sexual experiencing flows freely. (This can take longer with a couple with little or no prior sexual experience.) It usually takes a new wife that long to have a complete orgasm, although during the initial learning process she doesn't realize her experience is incomplete if she is in love with her husband and feels stimulated sexually with some form of release.

As her sexuality grows and becomes more physically complete, she is overcome with the constantly new and expanding experiences. Also, even though she may be experienced in sexual fulfillment, there are always new and different adjustments with a new partner. It takes time for two people to adjust fully to each other sexually; we have seen that this is one of the reasons that sexual experiences, especially initial ones, should be set in the context of a loving relationship which will continue long enough for the adjustment to be complete and the full benefit derived.

Mutuality of timing brings by far the most extraordinary experiences; however, it is not essential. No two orgasms are ever alike, unless the couple has fallen into some kind of habitual pattern of intercourse. It is the ever-changing combinations and variations which give a couple's sexuality its ever-new and of-the-now aspect. And it is the Now aspect which enables the couple to drop past-time hang-ups and to let go of projections into the future. Each time other-time constraints are dropped in the moment of sexual feeling their constrictive hold on everyday life is weakened.

Simultaneity of orgasm, although it is to be aimed for, need not be regretted when not attained if the couple are loving, feeling, and experiencing. The point is the mutuality and depth of response. However, if mutuality of orgasm is desired, there are several ways to attain it. The first, and most obvious, is to bring the slower member of the couple, usually the woman, up to the same level of sexual excitement as her partner by means of manual or oral manipulation of erogenous zones, and particularly the clitoris, while the faster member slows down. With a little practice a couple can adjust their timing in this fashion so that their orgasms occur together.

Actually, the problem takes care of itself when intercourse is repeated several times. If the first time the man comes more quickly than the woman, then the next time he will be slower to respond, and she will catch up with him. It is usually the third time in a sequence which can be the most marvelously satisfying of all. This is perhaps more true for the woman than for the man. However, any unusual experience is shared by a loving couple: when an orgasm is extraordinary for one member of a pair it is usually extraordinary for both, because feeling together and experiencing in common are so much a part of successful sexual interaction.

Also, most women have a number of orgasms, or are

capable of a number, during one session of lovemaking. It is possible, when the man's erection lasts long enough, for his partner to have several orgasms. She is also able to have one through manual or oral manipulation, and then join her husband when he has his. And there is no problem about arranging mutuality of orgasm if there is simultaneous manual or oral stimulation of both individuals.

Simultaneity of orgasm — in fact orgasm itself — is at times highly overrated. An interesting phenomenon of which most men are unaware is that a sensitive woman, relating with the man she loves, feels his orgasm as though it were hers — whether she herself has an orgasm or not. Many women cherish most the feelings of flow and fusion with their partner; certainly all couples know the bliss of floating off into successive levels of cloudlike feelings together after the orgasm has occurred.

Women appear to have more levels of feeling with their orgasms, more of a spectrum of feeling, than men. This may be simply because there are more motor and sensory areas which respond to the climactic release in the woman: the clitoris, pelvic muscles, uterine muscles, abdominal muscles, and even a flow of blood specifically to the breast areas.* Both men and women share the rush of blood to the extremities and throughout the body as the climax is initiated, and the wonderful feelings of physical release. With both men and women the deep peace, contentment, and communion following satisfied sex are the remarkable times of openness and transcendental feelings.

Orgasm as a result of penetration, along with simul-

---

* William H. Masters and V. E. Johnson, *Human Sexual Response* (Boston: Little, Brown and Company, 1966).

taneity of orgasms, has been highly overvalued. This has led to tension and pressure in lovemaking and feelings of frustration and inadequacy following "unsuccessful" intercourse. Actually, no sex need be unsuccessful, provided the couple is willing to open themselves to feelings, to move toward sexual excitement, and to allow varying means of gratification.

The burden of the necessity for simultaneous orgasm is a heavy one, particularly when there is sexual difficulty. With cases of frigidity and impotence, the first step is to remove the pressure for orgasm completely and to strive for feeling; at the same time the focus of attention should be moved from the genitals (and all sex-manual-directed clitoral stimulation) to the solar plexus, which must be open before anything at all can begin to happen. Then as the feelings start to flow, hands will move almost on their own, tactile stimulation will join feelings in arousing sexuality, and there can be the more direct approach of genital stimulation.

Actually, the imperative for all successful sex is focus on love and feeling; let the sex take care of itself.

Also, one should not worry about temporary hang-ups or barriers or shifts seemingly away from freer sex. In the course of the most ideal marriage each of the couple will go through problems which manifest themselves as sexual difficulties (temporarily) in the form of frigidity, impotence, inability to ejaculate, premature ejaculation, and so on. These difficulties are usually merely reflections of life problems which the individual is working through, and should be treated as such and not as major life tragedies. There are also unsettling periods of readjustment of a couple when they work through dependency

and identity problems with each other and with the marriage, as we have indicated in the section on growth.

The point is not to panic or feel that the relationship
has run its course or that love has fled out the window as
a new identity between the couple tries to walk in the
door. Sexual problems when treated as *the* problem are
never solved as such; one must always get to the underlying difficulty and then move toward its resolution. What
is needed is openness and warmth — and almost above
all casualness and patience — with each partner helping
the other when help is asked for and desired. Each individual has the responsibility to speak up out of his or
her feelings, to say where he or she is, and to ask for
what is needed.

Sometimes, however, the block from past time, or the
relationship problem which is being negotiated, is so severe that unusual — and unorthodox in the conventional
sense — means are needed to break it. It is as though the
couple suffered from double doors that were doubly
locked — one on each side — and some sort of action
must occur from outside which will open one of the doors
so that the individual can then turn and open the door
for his partner.

The most common means of breaking such a deadlock,
other than a separation from each other which may or
may not work, is by means of experience with another
person, either by one or both members of the couple.
This is very sensitive and difficult territory and must be
approached with great gentleness and delicacy. With loving partners who want only the best for each other, there
should be relatively little difficulty, and the appropriate
way to work out the problem can usually be found.

When the need is legitimate and the means are appropriate, any pain is the result of old neurotic mechanisms, usually possessiveness. However, great care must be taken to keep pain to a minimum — in fact to avoid it if at all possible. The situation is usually safer if there is some sort of guide or mentor who can offer unbiased perception about the reality of the difficulty and the necessities of the situation. The problem must be *worked out* rather than *acted out*.

Solutions of double binds in sexual blocking differ: sometimes it requires a discreet affair of one member; sometimes a visit or two to an attractive call girl; sometimes interaction with another warm and loving couple; sometimes a ménage à trois; even an orgy could be helpful. Generalizations are impossible: each couple is unique and their problems are so specific and special to them that a unique and special solution is required. The one generalization that can be made is that the phenomenal rise of sexual experimentation reflects in some part the magnitude of the problem and the driving need to solve it.

We shall see more and more of variations in sex and multiple sexual experiencing in the years to come — like it or not. Within a decade the various practices will probably be more or less acceptable means of working out difficult sexual problems for loving and committed partners (and as a basis for sexual relearning for individuals with difficulties), whether church and state give formal blessings or not. It is foolish to castigate and deplore the coming sexual revolution; the revolution is here and we must make sense of it and try to understand the needs that are not being met and how to provide more effective solutions to the problems.

At this point something should be said about breadth of experience versus depth. Numbers have little or nothing to do with successful sex; it is not the experiencing of sexual relationship with many individuals which teaches the knowledge and makes possible the reality of sexual fulfillment; it is the experience of depth — of progressive levels of feeling and varieties of experience. This experience of depth is the most possible and the most probable with one beloved partner. Certainly, clinically in the psychotherapist's office, it is much easier to break down overcontrol against sexual experience (unless there is serious emotional pathology) than it is to work through promiscuity to the capacity for depth of relationship in conjunction with breadth of sexual experience.

It is possible that an appropriate sequence of committed relationships might lead to the same depth of experience and to even more breadth than is possible with one individual. This, however, is not promiscuity. Actually, it really depends on what is appropriate for the individual. After all, one person may go all through school in one location; another may find that he must move through a series of different schools in order to learn what he needs to know. It depends on how good the schools are, also. Only "life" and the deep unconscious know what the solution is for each person, and each case must find its own proper expression.

Masturbation

There is one addition to the sacrament of sex which has been lost too long in the folds of the black sheep: masturbation. Masturbation is a very pleasurable and valuable tool — in life, in sex, and in marriage.

Unfortunately, prejudice against it prevails despite modern knowledge about sex and its functions, despite enlightened and supposedly guilt-alleviating information, and despite the fact that almost everyone indulges in this gratifying activity — surreptitious and ashamed though they may be.

The onus which masturbation carries probably has roots back in racial survival. After all, pleasurable sex with oneself limits sexual encounters which could lead to conception; conception is the indispensable requirement for man's continuation as a species. So the burden of guilt which afflicts masturbation probably had its beginnings far back in man's necessity to produce a lot of children in order to survive.

Further, society's conventional attitude toward masturbation is punitive, varying more or less with the particular culture's attitude toward sex. For instance, during the lusty Elizabethan era, it was regarded with good humor but as a poor substitute — one which a man used when he was unable to do better. (Historically, women have not been taken into consideration much with respect to sex as they have had very few sexual rights and privileges until recently when industrialization and contraception began to free them.)

And here appears another unpleasant connotation for masturbation: in our western civilization there seems to be some sort of spurious connection between rejection and masturbation. Those who indulge seem to experience feelings of inadequacy aroused by having no partner with whom to tango. Why should anyone, particularly a man, feel himself to be inadequate if he can't find someone to lay him? It doesn't seem logical, but the majority of people appear to feel that there is something wrong with them if they can't find a bed partner.

So — racial survival, and the coupling with rejection.

But there's more than that. Despite Freud, the latter-day freedoms, and the sex-love movement, we are still the product of our heritage. That heritage traditionally starts with symbolic Adam and Eve, who were thrown out of the Garden of Eden supposedly for learning about sex. It includes also a large element of the Puritan, topped off by Victorianism, which gave the feeling that not only was sex taboo but it wasn't even nice.

Insult on top of injury.

Furthermore, it was probably during the time of Queen Victoria that old wives' tales were concocted which held that masturbation certainly made a man impotent and probably drove him crazy. Grandmothers threatened little boys that they would "cut it off" if the little boy touched his penis. Of course in order to save him from an even worse fate.

Where could these wild inaccuracies have had their origin?

Our straitlaced forebears never stopped to think (and our repressed ancestors didn't dare) that any sort of emotional disturbance has its resulting reflection in the forceful, but sensitive, area of sex and reproduction. But why the threat of mental illness? Where is the connection between masturbation and mental illness? Probably it arose because of the overwhelming guilt associated with masturbation during sexually repressive eras. Another possible factor is the large amount of masturbation observed in conjunction with mental illness. Along with other inappropriate behavior and speech, masturbation is seen with disturbed children and on any ward of a mental hospital. However, the connection is by no means a causal one, although our guilt-ridden ancestors did not know this.

The truth of the matter is that masturbation is a very easy and pleasurable way of relieving anxiety and reducing tension and frustration, all of which are very prevalent concomitants of mental illness. Further, emotionally disturbed individuals do not have sufficient awareness of what is appropriate, nor do they have the necessary controls to restrain themselves from unacceptable behavior.

Inappropriateness of time and place has given masturbation a bad name. So has neurotic misuse. Obviously, out in public is not appropriate and — dynamically more important — the use of masturbation to lessen neurotic tension or fustration (which could be relieved in other ways) is damaging to the individual — just as are any other neurotic habit patterns which when pursued abort understanding and prevent solution of the problem. Normal individuals are able to function appropriately — to restrain themselves or to act when necessary, and to differentiate between the two. This capacity of appropriateness is part of the essential fabric of mental equilibrium.

The emotionally mature individual will not use masturbation inappropriately or neurotically. Masturbation can be a very hostile, destructive weapon when practiced instead of, or to the detriment of, sexual relationships with one's mate.

Another of the perils of masturbation is that it is so easily distorted by misuse as a vehicle for fantasies of an escapist or pathological nature. If a man becomes Don

Juan in his fantasies while masturbating in order to avoid relationship with women, he is not only doing himself the disservice of substituting fantasy for real life experience, but he is also conditioning a legitimate body-pleasure response to unreality.

With pathology, sadomasochistic practices can become so entrenched through masturbation that the individual is incapable of having a normal sexual relationship with another human being. Masturbation as escape or as fulfillment of emotionally sick needs is a distortion of the legitimate process of desire and of valid fulfillment. Also, it is possible that incorrect habit patterns and neurotic mechanisms, gaining strength from constant association with the forceful energy of the basic sex drive, can be conditioned and solidified into real pathology.

Then, too, masturbation is considered a particularly invidious form of sex because it can go undetected indefinitely — particularly with women.

All right, all right. Is there anything *good* to be said about masturbation?

Indeed there is. In fact, masturbation is possibly one of the most neglected means of growth and experience that we have at our instant command.

First, masturbation is a valuable technique for learning about sex — and about one's body. If our society were Polynesian rather than Judeo-Christian, children would learn about sex in free play with one another. Such is not the case; nor is free flow of information about sex possible in a society just a generation or two removed from suppressive sexual attitudes. Too many parents, despite wide dissemination of information, still have difficulty in speaking freely about sex, let alone masturbation. Even

in a society such as Sweden which is relatively free with
regard to sexual relationships, the same freedom with respect to one's self-stimulation and response does not generally apply.

Actually, masturbation is one of the best means we
have of learning about our own bodies and about sex
directly — without fear, hesitancy, guilt, or shyness. Since
all of the genital area is an erogenous zone, through masturbation one can discover the specific areas of greatest
sensitivity and the means and mechanisms of sexual re-
sponsiveness. One can also experience the rise of excitement and the release of tension into feelings of unity —
just as in sex with another person.

Secondly, it is an ideal means of sexual satisfaction
when there is no chosen or appropriate sexual partner,
or when the chosen partner is absent or ill. It is a sad —
and incredible — commentary on our society that masturbation has been frowned on more intensely than the
alternatives of prostitution and early promiscuity.

Thirdly, it is an excellent way of working through
sexual blocks — frigidity for women and inability to climax for men. When a woman has emotional barriers
which interfere with her letting go into full orgasm
(frigidity is one end-point in this spectrum), masturbation — both alone and with the aid of her sexual partner
— are the fastest means we have found (clinically) for
working through these blocks.*

* (Excerpt from letter of patient of author's who needed masochistic
fantasies in order to have sexual orgasm) ". . . Last night I masturbated
prior to retiring and thought how silly to have orgasms from being
hurt when I should be able to have one through being happy. So I
thought this and saw in my mind some lovely trees and hills. Then

The simplest aspect of the problem is getting used to letting go sexually — getting rid of the feeling that sex is bad and that one's body should say "No!" all the time. With enough practice and the desire to solve the problem, barriers rapidly disappear.

With men, the delayed climax usually has feelings of inadequacy at its root. With practice in masturbation, a man can learn to time his ejaculation — learning what will help him shorten the period by experimenting with sensitive areas and specific movements. Also he can learn to hold control longer, if his partner arouses more slowly, by avoiding the more sensitive areas at the beginning of love play. As with all human relationship — but particularly with sex — timing is of utmost importance, and it is through repeated efforts and practice on one's own that timing can be regulated when one is making love with another.

Also, masturbation can be used to help alleviate over-

I thought of L. and this produced colors — balloons and flowers — but I still couldn't climax. So I thought of B.S. and B.M. and E.E. and then I felt I could go through a happy orgasm. Still couldn't so I thought of G. and F. and you [therapist] and by that time I was seeing such lovely things in my mind . . . streams and wonderful green parks and bright color patterns of every description. Still no orgasm. So I knew I had to switch to being a hurt thing to finish, but this time I switched to being a very small girl . . . an ether or oxygen mask on my face . . . and went through the actual climax . . . I even felt the cutting vertically up my stomach [the patient had had a very painful abdominal operation as a child of about four]. After the climax I sat up and screamed the most anguished scream I have ever felt, but no sound came out. Then I started to sob. I felt a depth of anger that is being carried in me like a big blob caught in my diaphragm. I asked K. if she minded if I yelled into my pillow, which I did, until I began to get hoarse. And I started coughing deeply trying to get the bad things up. I am right on the whole mess [where] . . . I got mixed up in adolescence with the orgasm-hurt syndrome from childhood."

control mechanisms which were set in at too early an age. For instance, most older adults of this generation were toilet trained too soon and too rigorously (before ideas like Dr. Spock's had wide distribution). When the child has been trained in this fashion, the early, too rigorous, anxiety-surrounded control mechanisms generalize from the urinary (and anal) into the genital area.

With generalization, differentiations are obscured, and the process of holding on is set in for the entire pelvic area. This inhibition and resistance toward letting go of controls is impressed with top priority programming at a cellular level — and becomes very difficult to change. It is almost as though when sexual controls start letting go "all the way" a general alarm bell rings. The little girl part of the woman and the little boy part of the man is unable to discriminate what area the signal is coming from, and a tight control system goes into effect with STOP ALL ACTION having top priority.

"Letting go" is misunderstood by the body as that "terrible" situation of early pants-soiling or bed-wetting plus the wrath of an overly compulsive and punitive parent; the stop order takes effect with the unhappy result that full release of a sexual climax is not attained. It has been interesting to observe how many late maturing boys who were also bed wetters almost to their teens suffer from delayed orgasm or the incapacity to let go at all without complicated ritualistic acts.

In order to reverse overcontrol rapidly for a woman, an effective technique, therapeutically, is simultaneous masturbation and urination — of course under prepared conditions. With several repetitions, women are able to make distinctions between the sexual and urinary functions, thus undoing the confusion of early childhood training. This differentiation between the two areas and the two functions and the two letting go's helps remove the blocks, and the woman can move on to freer sex.

The discrimination of urinary from sexual feelings helps both men and women differentiate between involuntary sexual stimulation such as that from a full bladder (cf. "piss hard" erection for a man) and actual sexual desire. And, although the biological situation is different for men because of the single channel for discharge of both urine and ejaculate from the body, insightful and aware masturbation can also help a man discriminate between the two sources of stimulation.

Masturbation is also an excellent means of working on fears of inadequate sexual functioning — such as impotence and premature ejaculation. Full sexuality takes practice and experience. After all, one is not able to ride a bicycle on the first attempt; sexual skill, with all sorts of emotional and psychic factors present, is far more complicated than the coordination needed for bicycle riding. Fulfilling sex takes not only true feeling but also practice, and with masturbation one can practice opening up feelings and understanding (and mastering) the techniques of sex without the complications of trying to deal with a partner while still tentative and inexperienced.

But one should not stop there. Just as masturbation can help an individual find out about his own body, so can it help him to learn more about the body and sexual responses of his partner. The more sensitive, loving, *and* experienced two individuals are, the more deep and varied the sexual response.

People who recoil from any form of sexual expression

between loving partners other than "straightforward" intercourse reveal a limitation of their sexual openness. It is not that variations and embellishments, including shifts of position, should be in constant usage; it is just that there should be an openness to experimentation and variation whenever both members of the couple feel like it.

In conclusion, there is another function of masturbation — perhaps potentially its most important one. Certainly it is unique among faculties given to man that here is the one physical activity which can bring him to integration. Through masturbation a human being can move directly — through desire by way of will and physical action — to unity of the physical, emotional, and psychic. Masturbation, when accomplished appropriately, brings these aspects together in an experience which transcends any of the separate elements involved. And which also transcends duality.

Where else can one find a mystic or unitive experience — body, mind, and feeling — under direct control of the will?

In this Atomic Age of Anxiety — in these times of conflict and strife — unity of spirit is an all too rare occurrence. It has always been rare — so rare that this integrative experience is sought through religion in the churches, through sex in relationships of all kinds, through alcohol in social interaction, and today (as in the past but increasingly today) through drugs by certain groups and individuals — in any and all of these and other varied and numerous methods of self-transcendence through which man has sought unity and peace of mind from the beginning of time.

It is truly "holy" or "whole" to be at one with oneself.

Furthermore, it is the prerequisite for being one with another. It is impossible for a human being to be one with
another until he has experienced his own inner unity. It
is truly extraordinary to have a method available for experiencing unity with oneself so that one may experience
and learn and then move on toward experiencing unity
with another — an experience which is so much fuller
than he can manage by himself. Certainly the transcendental which one can experience sexually by oneself
through masturbation is but a pale shadow of what is
possible with a loving partner in a sacramental or committed relationship.

This brings us to words of warning and two bewares:
beware of guilt; beware of fantasy.

First, guilt — that forced and unwelcome handmaiden
of sex from earliest beginnings of Adam's self-conscious-
ness. As we have seen, the low and lewd character of sex
was one of the Puritan tenets; with them the dishonor
was probably refined to its ultimate. Victorianism ap-
propriated the debasement, combined this with tales of
romantic love, and conventionalized the mélange for
middle-class consumption. Not only was sex considered
tainted and usually evil; it was done only in darkest night
and under heaviest covers — for the good of the propaga-
tion of mankind.

Fortunately, the concept of the unconscious and the
knowledge of developmental stages and personality dy-
namics has scuttled the part of middle-class morality
which put such an onus on sex. However, because our
fathers were not entirely free, we are just emerging into
freedom ourselves. Guilt does exist; and neurotic guilt
plagues one's sexual experience.

The "straightforward" practice of sex has mostly extricated itself from the shadow. It has been slower for masturbation.

Further, there is the guilt that the unconscious masochist feels when he is called upon to enjoy himself. Pleasure still has a vaguely tainted air in our present-day world, and often an individual feels guilty about enjoying himself too much. Alas for the dregs of Puritanism.

To be forewarned should do the trick. Dump the guilt! The very practice of appropriate masturbation will help with this. How silly to find shameful something which was built into our bodies! And, if we are able to transcend the problem of guilt we also solve the difficulty of the age old put-down of the body — the canard that flesh is evil and only the spirit is exalted. How foolish not to love, honor, and cherish all parts of ourselves — mind, spirit, *and* body — and how sad if we do not avail ourselves of all the joy and pleasure possible with the instruments we were given. After all, our bodies are the third-dimensional event in space-time without which our minds, feelings and spirits would have no base or basis for existence.

If there is trouble with guilt, always remember that guilt is not possible where there is love. Sex flourishes and finds its highest and widest expression in the atmosphere of love. In the loving of another the first falling away of guilt-from-sex occurs. For freedom from the tentacles of neurotic guilt, how much must we love ourselves in order to be able to masturbate meaningfully?

Or, conversely, how much must we practice meaningful sex — masturbation included — in order to come to love ourselves? It is possible that the very process of masturbation can help us toward true self-love — self-acceptance — if not directly, at least by bringing to awareness those factors which prevent that acceptance.

However, if fantasy is imposed on masturbation, there will probably be a skew in the fullness of experience and in the learning and growth possible. There will certainly be not only bias but also destructive harm if neurotic or pathological fantasies are used, as has been mentioned. It is important to underline the fact that even everyday common garden-variety fantasy is likely to limit the experience.

With masturbation, as with sexual intercourse — or actually as with any deep interpersonal interaction — one should be open to anything which arises. Fantasy prevents openness. It should never be used in any sexual act because it imposes an immediate and almost insurmountable barrier: it shifts the experience from the now to past time (for what are fantasies but fossilized records of past time or crystallized wish fulfillments which one replays again and again?); and it interposes unreality on a situation which should be the height of the experience of reality.

So — let go of guilt and step aside from fantasy.

Masturbation is a very useful tool to help us toward fuller sexuality — and toward unity. We should use it delicately — and wisely — and well — as one part of the sacrament of sex.

12

Joy and Fulfillment

GROWTH in sexuality — sexuality itself in all its fullness — can only be had by experiencing in the now.

Everything we *experience* is in the moment, and it comes to us by way of our senses. Sensory experience is immediate; it cannot be manipulated either forward or backward in time without losing its fire and fragrance — without becoming a pale reflection of that which was.

It is impossible to feel hungry for tomorrow — or high for yesterday; feelings of yesterday and tomorrow are only echoes of an event which registered on our senses — echoes of the past or echoes of echoes (projections into the future). We choose to live in memory-past or memory-projected-into-future because we are afraid of being fully committed today — because we are terrified to let go fully to the now.

Past-time memories from before, or attachment to the previous, divert experience, changing it from the flow of a river to a hopscotching from known to known. The misuse of future time catapults one over the river in projecting forward from past time. Both serve as escapes from the moment of experience — from that which is.

The great value of sexuality is the immediacy of pleasure — the nowness of feeling. It cannot be skewed by past time in the form of fantasy or problems and remain an integrated totality. Sexual experience comes into being and expresses itself in the now of timeless feelings.

It is as we let go to sexuality that we learn to let go to the now. This occurs most easily in a relationship of love. Trust walks hand in hand with love, and in a relationship of love and trust we can open up to experiencing sensuality and sexuality and to feeling fully in the now. Herein lies the heart of marriage as an ongoing committed relationship whereby two loving partners learn progressive opening and trusting and experiencing in the moment.

However, progressive letting go in life can also occur within the framework of a meaningful life of integrity. Stability and order in our life and past experience provide trust of overall order in the universe. This allows an individual to let go even in those cases in which the person must remain open to the terror of progressive levels of the unknown.

Faith consists of the knowledge (or feeling) that this is an ordered universe, and that if we take one appropriate step after another we will arrive at a solution of the problem or our destination — and eventually at both. It is only when we feel that the universe is inconsistent and follows irrational impulses rather than orderly laws that we are without faith and are subject to free-floating anxiety. With an inconsistent universe, no matter how hard we work to take one appropriate step after another toward the solution of the problem, it would be merely a matter of chance whether we arrived at our destination or not. The inconsistent universe is too often a mirror of the child's first experience of the universe within a neurotic family circle.

If one has not had the experience which creates faith in the orderliness of the universe, the next best substitute is trust. In a relationship with someone I love I am willing to take a step into the unknown on the basis of trust in my beloved and in his or her faith that this is an orderly universe and that one can move toward fulfillment by putting one foot in front of another.

"A journey of a thousand miles begins with a single step," says the old Chinese proverb, but I must have faith enough to take that first step, or lacking faith, at least I must trust.

Not only love but also respect and admiration enables trust. Great teachers build bridges of trust for their students so that in going step by step across the bridge the student learns that one can take progressive steps in logical sequence and arrive at one's destination and that the universe is indeed orderly. In this manner basic anxiety is conquered, leaving only specific anxieties which can be dealt with more easily.

Besides the faith of inner knowledge, or the trust instilled by outer experience from one we love or admire, there is also the confidence and strength that a structured life can bring. If one is committed to and moving toward the goal of fulfillment of potential, there is a strength of action which allows steps into the unknown. Because I know in which direction my goal lies and because I am dedicated to taking every appropriate step to reach there, with each step I take I build a progressive network of confidence in order and in the orderly progression of cause and effect. This network serves as a structure of strength to guide my footsteps and contain my difficulties. If it is based solidly on reality and I am moving toward my potential, I am building a universe of integrity for myself and one in which my identity is clear. With the solidity of foundation and the integrity of an individual in motion toward his destination, steps can be taken without anxiety which otherwise would appear to be leaps into an unknown abyss.

The process of life — to be creative — must be two-fold: there must be the stability, the solidity, and the integrity; and then there must also be the freedom and the spontaneity wthin that structure. Just as in the process of creativity, there must be the spontaneous, and there must be the controlled.

With creativity, the flow must come unhampered from the unconscious; then critical faculties can impose pattern and structure. If the critical faculties are invoked too soon, the creative flow is choked off; if creativity pours out endlessly, results never materialize from the massive outflow which inundates structure and communication. With respect to life, the process is reversed: once structure has been established the individual feels free to let himself (or herself) go into completely spontaneous action, safe in the knowledge that commitment and structure will contain the unconscious expression within manageable bounds.

A basic paradox of living is involved: in order to be completely spontaneous I must be completely structured; in order to be free, I must be totally committed. Paradoxes exist because they do not take account of difference of reality level or of time — time which at the core of its reality is an illusion. But, being biological entities, we are subject to that illusion. So how best are we to move toward freedom of living, fulfillment of our potential, and creativity (which in the essence are all the same thing)?

It is in the doubly committed relationship — in the commitment to the one we love and to the relationship which will lead us both toward the fulfillment of our potential — that we are best able to absorb the lessons of the orderly universe, of commitment and structure, and of progressive freedom from limitations. It is as we love, and loving, take action for ourselves, for the one we love, and for the relationship of love we share, that we are able to have experiences of progressive freedom from restraints — freedom of our person, freedom from the invalid elements of society and culture, and finally freedom to experience fully in the universe as part of its awesome totality.

This voyage in love with the one we love is one of exploration and discovery as well as motion toward maturity. Sexuality within the context of such a voyage (within the context of a committed relationship) is the surest method available to complicated and vulnerable human beings to insure success along the way and in reaching the destination.

And joy should be the by-product of the voyage.

Joy comes hard to modern man. He knows pleasure; he knows ecstasy; he knows contentment and fulfillment. But joy is a stranger to his hearth because joy transcends the opposites and the hearth of modern man is built four-square on divisiveness and duality.

It is very difficult for us to allow ourselves to experience joy; we are so conditioned to the dichotomy of pleasure and pain that our sense of inadequacy and false abnegation conspire to dictate that we do not deserve to be joyful. The last, most difficult pattern to excise (or exorcise) from an individual undergoing character analysis is his reluctance to experience joy. It is as though there were some built-in prohibition against it in our culture: man feels that he cannot possibly deserve joy, or that he may achieve it only under certain difficult circumstances over which he has no control.

What a faulty perception of reality!

Joy and abundance are not only two of man's inherent birthrights, they are actual imperatives of life. If we do not achieve joy and abundance, we are not filling our potentials fully. Our task is to find out how to attain joy and abundance, to discover any barrier that may stand in our way, and to remove it. We are able to measure very quickly where we are in life by taking stock of how much joy and abundance we are experiencing.

However, life is a process; it is not a journey with a fixed destination. It is a way; and it is the process of life itself as we live it which is the way. This gives rise to the apparent paradox that if we seek reward, as in a goal (contentment, rest, surcease from burdens, or even joy and abundance), we immediately deflect ourselves from the possibility of its attainment. Having a known and specific goal is a limitation itself and imposes a complete predetermined sequence of steps. Having a sequence of steps which must be followed limits alternatives, imposes rigidity, and destroys spontaneity. A specific goal is known, and is a projection formed from our past experience. Compared to the infinite or unknown, our experience is infinitesimally limited, and in imposing a known or predetermined goal, we automatically and immediately impose a limitation on ourselves and create a barrier to complete fulfillment of our potential.

The focus must be not on the goal, but on the process. It is only as we are committed to the process (the way), which must always arise from and center in the immediate now, that direction can develop creatively from all the alternatives — known and unknown. Each step will then determine the next step in the sequence, and the sequence will lead to the goal. In the process we must manage two seemingly impossible and irreconcilable tasks: we must plan and order in time and we must live in the now, which is timeless.

If we set out toward a specific objective and force our choices toward its attainment without openness to all alternatives at each step, we shunt ourselves off onto a side road. If we continue on the side road, we end up in an alley. If we continue in the alley, we end up against a blank wall.

Of course, given a blank wall, we have the opportunity to decorate it with bright scenes of forests and oceanside — or even God — in order to prevent our recognition of what it is.

Painted scenes, however, do not change the reality of a dead end. Any specific and specified destination which we seek merely for our own pleasure — or use — halts us there, the ends having limited the means and then aborted the goal.

In order to be extricated, we must recognize that maturity is a process, just as life is, and not an end point. The commitment must be to continuous change and to taking action in whatever way is indicated from the prior step for the accomplishment of whatever needs to be done in the next one. In this fashion the process is created out of itself, and the motion becomes its own matrix for continuation.

God, as our finite minds conceive him, is *not* pleasure (when all else is meaningless I trust only my own senses), and God is *not* love (God is *all* emotion — all the colors in the spectrum, not just light blue); he is not Known of Known (how can the finite "know" the infinite); he is not a preset goal or a preordained lap of luxury for our future indulgence. God is change — probably nothing more, nothing less — and the only true commitment to "God" is a commitment to growth and fulfillment of potential. The path to meaning and meaningfulness in a universe which is in the shift from an expanding to a contracting universe is the process of commitment to change.

Why do we strive so hard to avoid change?

Change can be very painful. Only the masochist chooses pain over pleasure. However, the wise man chooses what is right for him; pleasure and pain become secondary considerations until one has progressed far along the road.

Actually change can be not only tolerable, but the way of growth, which involves continuous change, can become a joy with the right companion. The right companion is one who walks the committed way with us and shares not only each step in the process but also the direction and the goal, and is so in tune with us that the journey is turned toward gladness just by the fact of his companionship.

A companion along the way is necessary for very practical reasons as well as for pleasure. When we walk the path alone, there is danger of our mistaking the spark of a momentarily kindled flame for the light of awareness; there is too much possibility of the hearing of other voices and mistaking them for the still, small voice. Further, there is the danger of misperceiving the picture of how we would like things to be for the actuality of that which they are; and there is the ever-present danger of losing the image of ourselves in our admiration of its reflection in the pool.

A person needs the reflection of another event in space-time (*not* his own image); he needs an individual with whom he is companionable and who is traveling along the same path. No matter how short a space of time the two paths become one, each traveler serves as a reality point for the other, provided there is an understanding of what the relationship is to be, and what goals lie within its purpose. These determine the duration of the companionship, and if it be for only an hour, then for that time our traveler has enjoyed the refreshment of communication, the nourishment of relationship, and the strength of a checkpoint for reality.

How beautiful if our companion walks far along the way with us. Life's difficulties lose their rigor and can become like the joyous games and play of children when we are traveling with one we care for. How much better when the companions who are drawn together mesh on many levels; how incredible when they both mesh with each other and love.

We have touched briefly on the phenomenon of meshing in our discussion of the doubly committed relationship and of cellularly magnetic attraction. In fact, meshing was first mentioned in speaking about love (or absence of barriers) between individuals. This absence of barriers is most likely when there is deep feeling and affection between two people, and is further most probable when a couple is walking along the same path toward the same goal.

The importance of meshing, with respect to love, is that the more levels on which two individuals meet each other and fit together (physically, emotionally and psychically), the greater the possible range of fulfillment in the relationship.

To be more specific, meshing, in the sense in which we are using it, means to engage and form a pattern — to fit together. There are many forms and many fits possible in the variety of human differences and their interaction. But the closer the fit when a couple join, and the more levels which engage in union within a larger unity, the greater the meshing, and the more dimensions and infinities of relationship.

The levels and dimensions of meshing are as measureless as man's own variation. For instance, there are meshings of environmental similarity, of intelligence and education, of racial heritage, of psychological makeup, and — of utmost importance — meshing at a cellular level, which can seem to produce actual fusion of the two individuals. This is not only psychological fusion where the two people seem to be one, but actual, deep-level fusion where there appears to be physiological interpenetration in all areas.

There are also meshings within and without the context of space-time; meshings from the past where there might have been a similarly fulfilling relationship, or perhaps an unfulfilled relationship which remains to be completed; meshings from future time and because of common destinies which the two individuals have in common; and probably most important, the potential for meshing beyond time.

Meshing beyond time involves several elements: common destiny; mutual levels of openness; similar commitments (which are at one with reality and thus are functionally one single commitment); and that cellular fusion which occurs with such overwhelming pervasiveness and joy that it is as though the two individuals and the two separate bodies become the "one flesh" of the Bible.

When a couple mesh and fuse on the cellular level as well as the psychological it is as though two halves have joined together to become a whole, and the experience is one of unity which is contained within space-time and yet transcends it.

The finding of such another half of one's self is the miracle of relationship. If this miracle is to be, it occurs for two individuals only after they are deeply committed to life, to growth, and to the fulfillment of their potential — which may well take much time. If time stretches back farther than we realize, it may take more than a few lifetimes to find the one with whom we mesh completely, transcending space and time.

Probably one reason so few people find their other "transcendental" half is because they do not recognize him in person. In our society we judge each other by the superficials of appearance, dress, manners of speech, displayed intelligence, and overt talent and accomplishments. It takes time and an examination of deeper levels of attraction and potential to discover life partners, and it is virtually impossible if one is not committed to the fulfillment of one's own potential first. Often the right person for the long term (from the aspect of our own potential) is not the same individual one is drawn to for the short term. Superficial lack of attraction can keep a likely couple separated just enough so that any potential of deep physical meshing has no opportunity to manifest itself.

The most direct route to the discovery of one's lifetime companion is through the committed relationship. Another possible way to find the long-term partner is to work out divergences between two individuals who have been brought together through an overwhelmingly coercive physical attraction — working out the difficulties of intervening conflict.

Each of us must commit ourselves to growth — to change toward maturity and to the removal of all barriers which prevent us from fulfillment of our potential and of life's purpose for us. Implicit in this growth is the evolution of consciousness. The double commitment is that we commit to this for ourselves, for our mate, and for the relationship.

Man's task is to find out how to attain joy and abundance or, more accurately, to discover what stands in his way. The appropriate and committed use of the sacrament of sex (set in the matrix of a committed relationship) — meaningful sex between loving partners and also creative masturbation — is one of the royal routes for man. When sex does not take place with joy and a feeling of abundance, it not only can indicate the difficulty and designate the medicine for correction, but sex itself is also one of the best means we have for removing those limitations which prevent creative fulfillment. The full experience of sexuality (which at times becomes the way itself) can be a gloriously rewarding accompaniment to the process of continual maturation of the individual.

We must take note, however, that the road to one's fulfillment is hard and steep and rocky. There are times when the pain is virtually intolerable, even when we are in the company of the one we love. There are also times when our companion becomes intolerable to us, and the pathway appears to be impossibly steep and tortuous.

But eventually there is a change. As the couple pass more and more points of difficulty, as they negotiate more and more of the inadequacies and dependencies and interlocking problems of past time, joy in the process quickens. A second wind is found for the climb; burdens which had seemed to be of impossible weight suddenly take wing; and the two travelers are able to look toward the sky and many times to "be" where they are going. The levels of sacramental commitment of sex form a sequence paralleling different steps along the way: the initial experiences of youth; the ongoing relationship of growth; the more extended commitment for procreation; and the lifetime commitment to our companion for the journey toward the goal.

The real function of the committed ongoing relationship whose restricted present form we know as marriage is to help take individuals along the way together and to carry them beyond the points of difficulty of neurotic complexes and confusion.

The true purpose of marriage (aside from its initial responsibility for the continuation of the race) is as a means by which a couple can walk more safely and more swiftly — and with rising joy — along the road toward fulfillment of their own creative potential, thereby fulfilling their human potential.

The fact that marriage does not perform its function is not necessarily a reflection on the relationship between a man and a woman; it is far more a condemnation of the accretions of centuries and the limitations of lack of awareness which have grown like barnacles over the attempt to institutionalize and contain (legally and formally) the relationship potential between two human beings.

In this time of rapid change, of lethal overpopulation, and the rush toward self-annihilation, it is of critical importance to resurrect marriage (and sex), wash it with the waters of clarity, and restore it to its proper sacramental function in the maturing of man and the evolution of his consciousness.

And may there be continually increasing joy along the way.

74018